The Altitude Effect

The Altitude Effect

A Step-by-Step Guide to Setting Bold Goals, Rising Above Challenges, and Soaring to New Heights

Yvonne Heffernan

Paperback ISBN: 978-1-966659-41-9
Hardcover ISBN: 978-1-966659-42-6
Digital ISBN: 978-1-966659-43-3

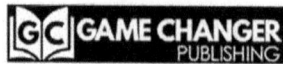

GC GAME CHANGER
PUBLISHING
www.GameChangerPublishing.com

Dedication

Dad, you showed me how to stand tall in the face of challenges, to embrace my power without fear, and to see failure as part of the journey, not the destination. I know you've been guiding me along this journey, and I imagine you in heaven right now, savoring a glass of red wine and celebrating this book's success :)

And to Ty, my little superhero: you make every day brighter with your jokes, your hugs, and your big heart. This book is for you—because you inspire me to never give up. Now that I've finished my book, I'll face my next challenge—winning a Fortnite Victory Royale with you. Ready up!

Read This First

As my way of saying thank you for buying this book, I've created a set of powerful resources to help you turn the book's strategies into real results!

Scan the QR code below to access *exclusive* ready-to-use worksheets/templates, inspiring video lessons, a guided 7-day challenge to jumpstart your goals, AND private access to a community built to help you win!

The Altitude Effect

A Step-by-Step Guide to Setting Bold Goals,
Rising Above Challenges,
and Soaring to New Heights

Yvonne Heffernan

"It is not the critic who counts; not the man who points out how the strong man stumbles, or where the doer of deeds could have done them better. The credit belongs to the man who is actually in the arena, whose face is marred by dust and sweat and blood; who strives valiantly; who errs, who comes short again and again, because there is no effort without error and shortcoming; but who does actually strive to do the deeds; who knows great enthusiasms, the great devotions; who spends himself in a worthy cause; who at the best knows in the end the triumph of high achievement, and who at the worst, if he fails, at least fails while daring greatly, so that his place shall never be with those cold and timid souls who neither know victory nor defeat."

–Theodore Roosevelt

Table of Contents

Introduction

Have you ever found yourself daydreaming about taking a safari in Tanzania or admiring the majestic icebergs in Patagonia? Skiing down the slopes of Aspen or basking in the sun's glow in Cabo? Maybe you've dreamed of climbing to the top of the Eiffel Tower or lying under a waterfall in Fiji. If you're like me, maybe you've dreamed about—or even completed—all of those!

What goes through your mind when you think of accomplishing each of those visions? Do you think, *Piece of cake!* Or do you immediately start to spiral and feel overwhelmed with everything you need to do to make each vision a reality: choosing the destination, booking the flights, and making all of the travel arrangements? If so, you've come to the right place! This book will remove some of the stress and overwhelm from the process of translating your vision into reality, including how to visualize, create goals (travel and otherwise), take action, and overcome obstacles along the way. If you're great at execution but have lost your joy and desire to dream, then this book is also for you. It will help guide you back to your North Star so that you can align your goals with your purpose and values.

Either way, you're in the right place. I've traveled to many of the destinations above, and hundreds of others. Some trips I've achieved with the help of my family and support system, and others I've achieved through my own hard work, planning, and execution. But in every case, the arrival at the destination came from visualizing the outcome, aligning it with my purpose, and executing it step by step until I had achieved my goals. In many cases, I had to overcome major obstacles.

MY STORY

I was born in Chad, Africa, to an American father and a French-African mother. My father met my mother while serving in the Peace Corps, where he worked on a water well project in N'Djamena. If you haven't heard of Chad before, it sits literally in the "heart" of Africa: a landlocked country in the very center of the continent, marked by extreme poverty, civil war, and plagued with limited women's rights, a lack of education, and child marriages. All of which is to say, my life didn't have to go the way it did, and it wouldn't have if it hadn't been for my father's decision to leave that life behind and risk everything to fly me and my brother to the United States.

While I don't remember the two *long* flights—spanning over 20 hours—from Chad to Washington, DC, my father made it a point to remind me how grueling it was as a single father (thanks, Dad!); how my brother and I refused to leave behind our two large teddy bears, which my father was forced to carry; how my brother loved to stick his fingers in the ashtrays that we walked by (back when you could smoke in the airport); and how we always managed to trip at the end of every moving walkway. Every. Single. One.

Thinking back on that trip with my father, I'm struck by the challenges he faced and the intricate planning it took to bring all of the moving pieces together. It's no exaggeration to say it was a small miracle that we all made it to DC (and with my dad's sanity mostly intact)!

Fast forward to six years ago, and my world was crashing down. Within six months, my father lost his battle with cancer, my marriage dissolved, and I became a single mother to a two-year-old. Grief, shame, and self-doubt consumed me as I faced the daunting reality of raising a child, paying for a $5,000 Brooklyn apartment by myself, and trying to rebuild my life from the ground up.

I had hit rock bottom (again). But in that moment of despair, I discovered something extraordinary: the power to rise was within me. I realized I didn't have to be perfect to rebuild. Vulnerability wasn't weakness—it was strength. And so, I began to confront my pain, channel my anger and sadness into fuel, and take bold steps toward transformation.

WHO I AM TODAY

Today, I stand as living proof that even the most shattered lives can be rebuilt into something extraordinary. I've reclaimed my joy, self-confidence, and purpose—and let me tell you, it feels amazing. I've thrived in Fortune 500 leadership roles, built a successful consulting business, and now, I coach people just like you to align their goals with their unique purpose. My mission is to help you take bold action, develop resilience, and create a life filled with joy and freedom.

Along the way, I've learned the power of community. I've surrounded myself with people who inspire me, make me laugh, and remind me that it's okay to be vulnerable. And yes, while I'll never claim to have everything figured out, I've mastered the art of setting audacious goals that align with my values and making them happen.

Along the way, I discovered the "secret sauce" that has helped me to transform my life:

1. Shifting your **mindset**.
2. Owning your **power**.
3. Setting bold **goals**.
4. Taking **action**.
5. Giving yourself **grace** (because you're human).
6. Grounding your life with **love**.

These principles aren't just theories—they're the foundation of *The Altitude Effect*. They're what helped me turn my life around, and they can help you, too.

HOW DID I GET TO WHERE I AM TODAY?

When I moved to the U.S. from Chad at the age of three (after our marathon flight), I didn't speak any English. Not one word. When my father used to pick me up from daycare and speak to me in French (my native language), I would pretend I had no idea what he was saying. Sorry, Dad. At age three, I was already headstrong, opinionated, and sassy, which would ultimately be both a blessing and a curse. Yes, it would sometimes get me in trouble, but it would also allow me to speak up and advocate for myself, negotiate for raises and promotions, and lead teams of hundreds of people toward shared success.

Like most people, I didn't have my whole life mapped out after college. I waitressed while I figured things out, eventually landing my first corporate gig as an Administrative Assistant at the Spina Bifida Association of America (SBAA). My first task? Track conference attendees. My solution? Spend the weekend with a copy of *MS Access for Dummies* and come back Monday as the office's unofficial tech guru. And so my tech career began.

Every step of my career—from Administrative Assistant to E-commerce Director to Founder—built on the one before it. In my professional life, I was focused, powerful and resourceful. So when life shattered six years ago, I tapped into that same resourcefulness. I created bold goals for myself: financial stability, a secure home for my son, and a life filled with purpose and joy.

But here's the thing—I couldn't find a single book that combined mindset shifts, goal-setting, and execution in a way that resonated with me. So I did what any determined, slightly desperate person would do: I created my own framework.

WHY DID I WRITE THIS BOOK?

They say you write the book you wish you had, and *The Altitude Effect* was the book I needed when I was lost, broken, and searching for a way forward.

My father's passing was the catalyst for me to refine this framework and honor the lessons he left behind. He taught me resilience, self-belief, and the importance of action. As I shared these lessons with friends and colleagues, I realized they resonated deeply because so many people feel stuck—trapped by limiting beliefs, fear, or life's circumstances.

So, ultimately, I wrote this book to help others break free. To show that no matter how overwhelming life feels, there is a path forward. I wanted to show them the framework I've used to rebuild my life, achieve financial freedom, and even pursue dreams like performing as a jazz singer and buying my own condo in New York. It's the same framework I've used to guide start-ups, start my own company, write a book, and implement strategies for global brands like LVMH and Christian Dior.

Through *The Altitude Effect,* I want to empower you to:

- Shift your mindset to see challenges as opportunities.
- Set bold goals that align with your purpose.
- Take meaningful action to create a life you love.

WHO IS THIS BOOK FOR?

The Altitude Effect is for anyone ready to rise above life's challenges and create a life filled with purpose, joy, and success. Whether you're finally ready to take action toward a long-held dream, or you're feeling stuck, overwhelmed, or uncertain about the future, this book is your guide to breaking free from the barriers holding you back.

It's for:

- Those with a vision but no clear roadmap to achieve it.
- People standing at a crossroads, unsure of their next steps.
- Anyone caught in a cycle of unfulfilling jobs, relationships, or choices and longing for a way out.

This book is also for those who feel trapped by corporate pressures but are scared to leap into the unknown, or for anyone feeling isolated, disconnected, and lacking the community or support system they need to thrive.

If you've been weighed down by grief, self-doubt, or guilt from past mistakes, this book offers more than hope—it provides a holistic framework to help you heal, grow, and move forward. Through mindset shifts, meaningful goal-setting, inspired action, and self-compassion, *The Altitude Effect* will empower you to embrace your journey, align with your true values, and define success on your terms.

WHAT WILL YOU GET OUT OF THIS BOOK?

The Altitude Effect isn't just a book; it's your personalized guide to transformation. Here's what you can expect:

- **Clarity and Focus:** Learn how to break free from limiting beliefs and adopt a mindset that turns challenges into opportunities. You'll discover how to focus on what truly matters, fostering resilience and a sense of control over your life.
- **A Proven Framework:** Gain access to a clear, actionable roadmap for success. From crafting a compelling vision to setting bold goals and executing them with confidence, you'll transition from a dreamer to a doer.
- **Redefining Success:** Embrace a new perspective on success—one rooted in love, vulnerability, and grace. You'll cultivate deeper relationships, align your goals with your values, and experience a more fulfilling, authentic life.
- **Empowerment and Motivation:** Leave behind the victim mindset and step into your power. With the tools and strategies in this book, you'll find the strength to move from stagnation to inspired action.

After reading *The Altitude Effect,* my hope is that you'll feel empowered, inspired, and equipped to create the life you've always imagined.

- You'll expand your view of what's possible, breaking free from the limitations that have held you back.
- You'll craft bold, meaningful goals that bring you closer to your dreams, fueled by the confidence to take action.
- You'll learn to stop judging yourself, replacing self-doubt with self-compassion.
- You'll build a life aligned with your deepest values—a life filled with joy, purpose, and freedom.

Most importantly, you'll realize you're not alone. You'll have the tools to transform setbacks into stepping stones, empowering you to embark on a journey of growth and fulfillment that's uniquely yours.

WHAT DO AIRPORTS AND FLIGHTS HAVE TO DO WITH ACHIEVING GOALS?

Beginning with my first flight out of Chad to Cameroon and followed by my first transatlantic flight to the United States, my life has been full of travel and adventure. Ever since my father instilled this sense of wanderlust at a very early age, I have traveled to five of the seven continents and continue to be amazed at the lessons I learn as I travel to new destinations throughout my life.

When I plan a new trip, the framework is the same, even though the destination, the clothes I pack, and the specific steps are different. In every case, I have to prepare for the flight, get onto the plane and into my seat, take off, and then arrive at my destination. What I've learned is that if any of those things fail to happen, chances are that I will not arrive at my destination on time, or at all. I've also learned a lot about myself, such as the resilience, strength, and tenacity that I have to finish the things that I start in the face of obstacles.

Because I'm passionate about travel and because the topics in this book can be quite dense, I've decided to use **airport** and **flight** analogies to make them more relatable, representing the preparation, planning, execution, and completion of your goals. Much like taking a trip, where you choose a destination, pack your bags, navigate each stage of the flight, and prepare for unexpected turbulence, your goals require thoughtful planning and the resilience to navigate challenges along the way.

Whether you have never taken a flight before or whether you're a fellow jetsetter, the concept is the same: You can arrive at the destination of your choosing by following the framework I'll provide in this book.

HOW THIS BOOK IS ORGANIZED

The book is organized into five parts. In **Part 1**, we'll cover all of the preparation that you have to complete before you even get to the airport (the execution). This includes being clear on your purpose, values, and goals. It includes ensuring your passport (skills/qualifications) is up-to-date and that you've packed the right items (beliefs). Lastly, it includes checking in and giving yourself the freedom to change/cancel your flight (goal)—if needed.

In **Part 2**, we'll cover everything you need to do before your dreams take off. We'll start with checking your passport & ticket. We'll discuss how to print your boarding pass (create objectives), get through security (let go of limiting beliefs), board the plane (kick off your goals), and find your seat (step into your power). Before and during takeoff, you'll fasten your seatbelt (commit fully), read the safety information card (mitigate potential hazards), release your fear of "flying," and create momentum to leave the ground.

In **Part 3**, we'll cover how to continue to gain altitude, set milestones, track your progress, and make in-flight adjustments (pivot) when needed. This chapter also reminds you how to leverage the "flight crew" (your support system) for assistance and refreshments (support and celebration). Lastly, we'll cover how to handle turbulence and prepare for a smooth landing.

In **Part 4**, we'll go over preparing for the descent and how to "touch down" (achieve your goal) smoothly. This includes celebrating your achievement, gathering your belongings (lessons from the experience), exiting the plane, and clearing customs (declaring what you have picked up along the journey).

Lastly, in **Part 5**, we'll cover obstacles that prevent you from getting to your final destination smoothly, including missed connections, flight delays, layovers, and crashes.

HOW TO USE THIS BOOK

To get the most from this book, I recommend reading the chapters in order since each chapter builds upon the previous chapter. You should also complete the exercises in order, as many of them also build on previous exercises. I recommend buying a journal to use specifically for completing the exercises in the book, or use *The Altitude Effect Companion Workbook*, designed exclusively to guide you on your journey. Think of this as your flight plan!

And most importantly, remember to take this adventure one step at a time, give yourself grace along the way, and *have fun!*

The Altitude Effect is more than a guide—it's your ticket to a life of bold goals, meaningful connections, and limitless possibilities. Let's take flight together!

TRAVEL CHECKLIST

- ***The Altitude Effect Companion Workbook -or- Notebook:*** *Scan the following QR Code to purchase* ***The Altitude Effect Companion Workbook!***

Would you rather use a notebook? My favorite type is the unlined artist notebook. You can find these at most bookstores or even Target/Amazon. You can even download and print the FREE bonus worksheets at the end of this book and glue them into your notebook.

- ***Colored Markers:*** *Who said goal-setting has to be boring?! This is your chance to bring your vision to life and draw your goals in color. I invite you to complete the exercises in color. Use different colors for different themes or goals, or just because you want to.*
- ***An Open Mind:*** *Let go of any preconceived notions about how this will go. Let yourself be open to the journey of exploring and executing your goals. You might even find yourself starting to enjoy it!*

Part 1:
Preparing for Your Flight

When you're preparing for your flight, it's the beginning of your journey and the most important part. You need to be clear about your purpose and your values and visualize your destination.

With that vision, you tap into your power to choose a flight that will transform your vision into reality. You take action and book the flight, committing to the journey. You ensure that your passport is up-to-date with the requirements to get you on the flight, and has enough "pages" to include arriving at your destination.

You choose your travel companions and pack for your flight based on your specific destination. You create an itinerary that will allow you to achieve each of the milestones that ensure a successful trip. Lastly, you check in and ensure that you're still aligned with your goal.

All of this happens before you've even gotten to the airport and boarded your flight. These steps help to create a solid foundation that gives you the best chance of achieving success.

Understanding Your Purpose

If you're booking a leisure trip with family, you're less likely to book a hotel in an urban location that caters to businessmen. Just as you can't choose a destination for your flight without first knowing your purpose, achieving success starts with understanding your purpose: what you want to achieve and how success aligns with that vision. Your purpose serves as a guiding pathway, grounding you as you navigate your journey and providing your life with direction, meaning, and fulfillment.

Maybe your purpose is to be a parent, to heal, or to teach. Maybe it's to inspire others and show them what's possible. Or maybe you're not quite clear on your purpose yet, and that's okay. Or maybe you were clear on your purpose 10 years ago, and now you find yourself searching for meaning. All of that is okay. Not only is it okay, it's part of life's evolution.

Throughout life, our purpose may change and evolve as we gain clarity on what's important to us, as we shift values and grow through different seasons of our lives, as we face and overcome obstacles, and as we experience growth and loss. There have been times in my life when I have lost my sense of purpose, and I've used the exercises in this book to regain my clarity and zest for life. I've used it to prioritize and channel my energy, to dig deep, and to motivate myself when facing overwhelming obstacles.

You may accomplish many things in life but still feel unfulfilled without meaningful purpose behind your actions. After years of hard work, you might find yourself asking, *What do I have to show for it?* For example, maybe you're in a career where you're miserable even though your achievements have been significant. You've received accolades and achieved milestones, but you still feel something's missing.

This may be a great time to revisit your purpose and ask yourself the question: *Is this career aligned with my purpose and my values?* When you set goals with a larger vision in mind, one aligned with your values and your purpose, things fall into place synergetically. That's not to say that every goal will use this approach. There are definitely times when opportunities find us, catch us by surprise, and all that we have to do is to say, "Yes." But for most of life, we create our own miracles when we put ourselves in the pilot's seat, choose our own destination, and take charge of our lives.

That said, you can have purpose no matter what your job is, whether you're a janitor, a teacher, an executive, or a CEO. It's about aligning your work with your core values and your unique contributions to the world. Because let's face it: Most of the work we're doing on a daily basis isn't profound, Nobel Prize-worthy work. But if we're able to engage in what is really important to us and make sure our needs are being met, then the work will still be fulfilling.

When you look back on your life, will you say, *I achieved all of these things, but I was miserable,* or are you going to say, *Wow, I really made a difference, and my life had meaning?* It's a completely different way to look at your life. But what's wonderful is that we have the opportunity to look ahead and say, *Maybe up until now, I haven't. Maybe I've achieved a lot in my life, but I haven't been fulfilled. And now I have the choice to look ahead at the rest of my life and do it differently. What life experience do I want to create for myself? Why am I here on this Earth?*

First, let's discuss a few ways to home in on your purpose:
- **WHAT** is the legacy you want to leave?
- **WHO** are the people that you feel most drawn to help?
- **HOW** do your talents/passions/contributions, and your work, intersect to show your unique contribution to the world?

For example, I know that my job as a mom is an important part of my purpose here on Earth. This has become even more pronounced since I became a single mother. I think about the generational wealth that I want to create for my son and the lessons that I want to teach him. I also know that I'm called to coach, inspire and lead.

Picturing Your Legacy

> *"Ask yourself today, in the middle of your complicated,*
> *demanding, chaotic life: What do I want my legacy to be?*
> *And then start living from that intention."*
> −Oprah Winfrey

Thinking about the legacy you want to leave for your family or future generations can be a powerful way to clarify your purpose.

THE 80TH BIRTHDAY/LEGACY EXERCISE

Imagine your family and friends surround you as you're celebrating your 80th birthday. After you blow out your candles (hopefully without spitting out your dentures, ha-ha), your family and friends speak about you and the impact you've had on their lives.

- *Who are you with?*
- *How do you feel?*
- *What do they say about you?*
- *How have you served your community and those around you?*

5-MINUTE REFLECTION: ALIGNING WITH YOUR LEGACY

- Which values are reflected in your future self?
- What is the legacy that you've created?
- Are you living in alignment with this legacy? If not, what is missing?

Identifying Your Ikigai

Once you have a general sense of your purpose, you can go deeper by identifying your *ikigai*, a Japanese concept that means "reason for being." Your ikigai sits at the intersection of what you're good at, what you're passionate about, what you can be paid for, and what the world needs.

IDENTIFYING YOUR IKIGAI (PURPOSE) EXERCISE

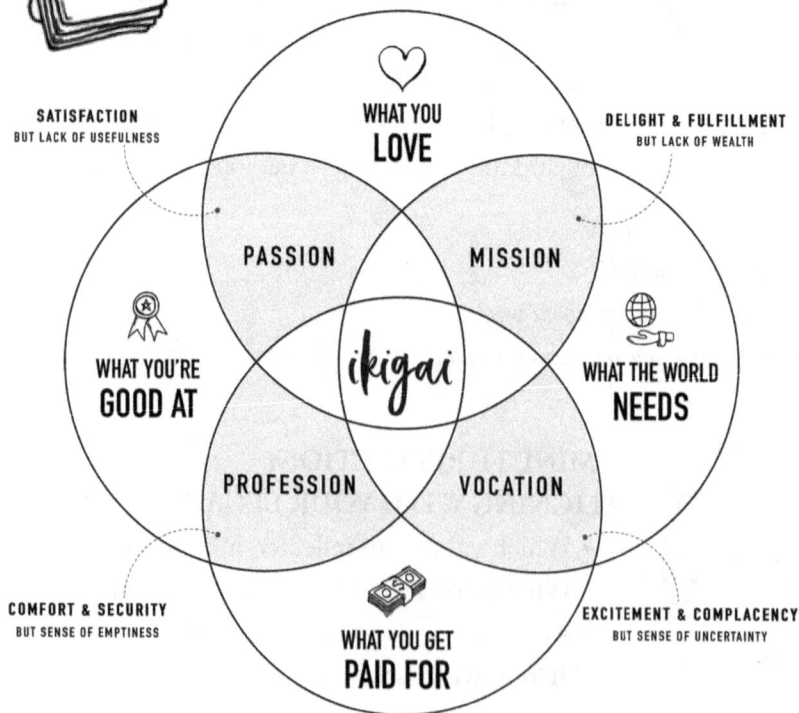

WHAT YOU LOVE

WHAT YOU'RE GOOD AT

WHAT THE WORLD NEEDS

WHAT YOU GET PAID FOR

PASSION

MISSION

ikigai

PROFESSION

VOCATION

SATISFACTION
BUT LACK OF USEFULNESS

DELIGHT & FULFILLMENT
BUT LACK OF WEALTH

COMFORT & SECURITY
BUT SENSE OF EMPTINESS

EXCITEMENT & COMPLACENCY
BUT SENSE OF UNCERTAINTY

1. Draw four overlapping circles representing the four ikigai categories:
   a. **What you LOVE doing** (your passions, what gets you out of bed)
   b. **What you're GOOD AT** (your skills and strengths)
   c. **What the world NEEDS** (how you contribute to the world)
   d. **What you can be PAID FOR** (your job/career)
2. Write down five responses within each circle for each category.
3. Look at areas where the four categories overlap. This is your **ikigai**, or **purpose**.

5-MINUTE REFLECTION: CONNECTING WITH YOUR PURPOSE

- Look at the areas of your life where only two of the categories overlap and check in with your feelings. Which feelings come up for you?
- Which areas of your life connect all four categories? How can you connect more fully to this purpose?

Defining Your Purpose

DEFINING YOUR PURPOSE EXERCISE
With the insights that you've gotten from the last two exercises, write down as many purpose statements as you can for each of the following four quadrants.

PERSONAL LIFE	PROFESSIONAL LIFE / BUSINESS
• Example: My purpose is to create a safe, loving, and nurturing home for my family **so that** they can make a positive difference in other people's lives.	• Example: My purpose is to create research that makes a difference in my field **and** paves the way for future groundbreaking discoveries.
PASSIONS / HOBBIES	COMMUNITY
• Example: My purpose is to create and perform music that inspires people **so that** their lives are enriched.	• Example: My purpose is to volunteer for a local non-profit **so that** I can help people who are less fortunate.

5-MINUTE REFLECTION:
ALIGNING YOUR PURPOSE WITH SERVICE
• Why are each of those purpose statements meaningful to you?
• How do each of those statements serve others and leave the world a better place than how you found it?

Researching the Terrain
& Places to Stay

Before deciding on a destination, you combine your purpose with the values ("terrains") that match the outcome you want to achieve. The destination ultimately represents your values and the type of experience you want to have once you arrive.

- Do you value peace and tranquility (a quiet beach vacation)?
- Do you value adventure and excitement (a jungle escape)?
- Do you value love and family (a family resort)?
- Do you value religion and spirituality (a trip to Mecca)?
- Are you looking to choose a destination you've been to before and expand upon it, or try something new?

Achieving success begins with defining what it means to you and making it tangible. What achievements constitute success in your life? What are your goals, and how can you measure your progress?

Ultimately, your success is defined by your unique values. What feels like success to one person might not resonate with another. That's why it's important to revisit your values on a regular basis and reassess how they show up in your daily life.

VALUES ASSESSMENT EXERCISE

Step 1: Review this list and circle the 10–15 values that resonate most strongly with you. If there are any that you think of that aren't in the table, feel free to add your own!

Adventure	Compassion	Boldness	Empathy
Creativity	Achievement	Community	Happiness
Kindness	Innovation	Curiosity	Honesty
Love	Growth	Fairness	Knowledge
Service	Fun	Religion	Leadership
Loyalty	Peace	Recognition	Respect
Responsibility	Security	Stability	Wealth
Trust	Status	Spirituality	Health
Authenticity	Learning	Optimism	Justice
Independence	Family	Humor	Integrity

Step 2: Put a star next to your top 5 CORE values and rank them (1–5), with 1 being the most important and 5 being the least important.

If you're having a hard time narrowing it down, look back at your answers from the last chapter regarding your purpose. Which themes jump out at you? It's important to narrow down your values and guiding principles so that you have an internal compass as you navigate success across different areas of your life. Also, be mindful that your values will change over time, and that's completely normal. That happened to me, as well!

5-MINUTE REFLECTION: EXAMINING YOUR VALUES

- Consider the different areas of your life. Where are you living in alignment with these values? Where are you out of alignment?
- How do these values manifest in your daily life?
- What have you learned about yourself through this exercise? Were there any values that surprised you?

Choosing Your Destination

Once you understand your purpose and values, the next step is to visualize your destination. This can be the trickiest part because some areas of the mind communicate through images rather than words. But if you can see it, you can have it.

It's vital to remember that choosing your destination is not about going somewhere everyone else is going, although you might be inspired by others' journeys and stories. It's about creating a vision that aligns with your unique goals, skills, and talents. Do you envision yourself sipping a Piña Colada in the pool of a Mexican villa, walking along the banks of the Seine, or zip-lining through the jungle of Costa Rica? Each of those destinations is wonderful, and maybe even part of different visions within your own life, but with each one comes a completely different set of itineraries, luggage, weather conditions, and experiences.

High-Altitude Hack: If you're struggling with making a decision between multiple options, the "Pros vs. Cons" exercise can be very helpful:

List each option in one column, and for each one, ask yourself the following questions:

- What are the pros and cons of this choice?
- What are the potential consequences/impacts of this choice?
- Am I willing to deal with these consequences/impacts?
- How does this choice align with my long-term goals or values?

At the end of the day, understanding your purpose and values gives you direction, but nothing happens until you create a vision that ties them together. When you combine the components into a cohesive picture that you can see in your mind and then create goals that allow you to fulfill the vision, something magical happens!

I've used this technique hundreds of times in my personal life: when rebuilding my life, moving to New York, performing as a jazz singer, landing a new job, negotiating a raise, buying a home, and paying off debt. In fact, when I was 28, I sat down and mapped out what I wanted to achieve over the next ten years. I had made sure to be as specific as possible. I wrote down goals like wanting to be fluent in French again, own my own home, pay off all my credit card debt, move to New York to perform with my band, and land a job making at least 25 percent more than my current salary. Notice I said "more than" 25 percent because a powerful vision statement doesn't limit you! If you set your sights on making $100,000, the universe might just hand you that amount and nothing more. Why box yourself in? By the way, I still have that paper! A few months ago, while cleaning and organizing, I stumbled upon it and realized I'd achieved almost everything on the list—except for one tiny detail. Talk about inspiration!

Keeping your mind open lets life surprise you in delightful ways. For instance, when I'm locked into my vision, taking action, and in alignment with my purpose, I start to notice all sorts of little gifts from the universe—like free passes to events, random coupons at the checkout, or even the cashier at Van Leeuwen treating me to a free ice cream because the person in front of me had a coupon. That's the universe's way of giving you a high five and letting you know you're on the right track!

At any given moment, you can design your own life because you alone have the power to create the life you want. You don't need permission from yourself or anyone. Sometimes, we know what we want, but we don't know how to visualize it, or where to start to create what we *do* want.

Other times, it's kind of a hazy picture, or a generalized view. The trick is to transform that hazy picture into a clear vision that you can execute against. This is when the "Magic Wand" exercise comes in handy. The concept is simple.

THE "MAGIC WAND" EXERCISE

If you could create the life of your dreams with a wave of a magic wand, what would that look like? No constraints, nothing holding you back, no loophole to let your mind think of why something couldn't happen. If there was no resistance, what would be possible? What would it actually look like?

Imagine when you wave that magic wand, you are transported into that vision in full surround sound and 3D high-definition color. Write down the vision that you see in your mind's eye.

- What are you doing?
- What environment are you in?
- How are you feeling?
- Which of your values are being fulfilled in this vision?

When I was 26 and lived in Washington, DC, I was living my best life. I was performing as a jazz singer throughout the DMV area. I was dating a stereotypically sexy saxophone player (I stumbled into that alliteration). Life was great! And then, sadly, we broke up. I was devastated. We had dreamed of getting married and moving to NYC to perform together. Now here I was, heartbroken and depressed, wondering how I could ever move on. I hit rock bottom.

But then, one day, as I was staring blankly into my coffee, watching my tears fall into the mug, I made a decision: enough was enough! Why couldn't I still have that dream? He didn't own it. It wasn't trademarked. It had been my dream, too. And it still could be!

So, I went to Barnes & Noble, bought a scrapbook, filled it with photos from a previous trip, and made a vision board with images I cut out from magazines—some of which didn't even make sense to me at the time. There was this subconscious guiding my choices, and that's where the magic happens! I vividly pictured my dream trip to New York: taking the train, strolling through Central Park, biking around Prospect

Park, and hitting up the farmer's market on a sunny Saturday morning. I created my own vision statement, which included working during the day and performing at night, and the type of work environment where I would thrive.

I also used vision boards to bring my vision to life! The best ones I've created were the simplest.

Flight Tip: Swing by CVS or your local drugstore for a poster board, then raid the bookstore for magazines featuring images of your aspirations. If you can't find any, no worries—order some glossy magazine clippings from Etsy! Personally, I love cutting out images myself, but you do you. Carve out a chunk of time to clip and paste everything for your vision board in one go. Otherwise, you'll end up with a pile of clippings buried under your couch or possibly pilfered by your cats (I'm just saying, speaking from a friend's experience).

At different times, I've also used apps and Pinterest to capture my inspiration. Remember, don't judge your selections; go with your gut and let those feelings guide you. After all, some things can't be expressed in words—they just resonate on a deeper level.

I also collected affirmation cards, reading them over and over. I'd stash them in my bag, pull them out on the train, and even save them on my phone. I think I downloaded every "Affirmation" app out there! My all-time favorite cards are still the classic ones by Louise Hay—durable and timeless; they always inspire me to keep dreaming and moving toward my goals. I created my own affirmations and wrote them every day as part of my morning routine.

You try!

VISION STATEMENT EXERCISE
Now take your vision from the above and use it to write down a vision statement using the prompts below:

1. **What do you HAVE?** This is the outcome, something tangible and measurable. It could be the amount of money in your bank account, a job title, a product, a relationship, a project, a certain weight, or a new address.
2. **What are you DOING?** What does your day-to-day look like that makes your vision a fulfilling experience?
3. **Who are you BEING?** How are you showing up as the best version of yourself? How are you being of service to others? How is this vision serving your highest self?

How can you support your vision with affirmations that sustain your commitment and motivation?

HOW TO CREATE IMPACTFUL AFFIRMATIONS

1. **Phrase the affirmation in the present tense.** Instead of writing in the future tense ("I will have a new job"), try "I am thriving in a fulfilling new job that brings me joy and growth."
2. **Write in the first person.** Instead of using a single word like "Peace," phrase the affirmation as a sentence in the first person ("I am surrounded by tranquility and serenity in every moment").
3. **Focus on the positive.** Instead of "I'm not in debt," try "I am financially free and in control of my finances."
4. **Don't limit yourself.** Instead of "I'm making $100,000," try "I attract abundant wealth and create multiple streams of income that exceed my financial goals."
5. **Focus on how you can contribute.** Instead of "I am a great parent," try something like "I nurture and raise compassionate, responsible children who contribute positively to our community."

Most importantly, repeating the affirmations on a daily basis helps to prepare your subconscious as you continue to take action on a conscious level.

NEXT STEPS:

1. Write five affirmations that will support you as you fulfill your vision.
2. Create your own vision board and post it somewhere visible.
3. Review both items daily!

Buying Your Ticket

The moment you fill out your information, add your payment information, and click "Submit" to buy your ticket, you say "Yes" to the destination, to the experience, and everything that comes with it. You reserve a "seat" on the plane traveling to your destination and take responsibility for your part in the outcome.

You commit to when you will start (the departure time) and when you will finish (arrival time). You commit to starting where you are now (your departure airport) and traveling to another destination in life (departure airport). You commit to taking action and showing up where and when you need to show up along the way to reach your destination.

And it all gets set in motion with that click of a button or a phone call. Life is the same way. Sometimes you will create your own opportunities; other times, the opportunity will present itself to you, and all you need to do is say, "Yes."

> *"Yes to everything scary. Yes to everything that takes me out of my comfort zone. Yes to everything that feels like it might be crazy. Yes to everything that feels out of character. Yes to everything that feels goofy. Yes to everything. Everything. Say yes. Yes. Speak. Speak NOW. 'Yes,' I say. 'Yes.'"*
> —Shonda Rhimes, *Year of Yes*

SAYING "YES" TO POSSIBILITIES

When I was a child, I loved the puzzle game Brain Teasers. Especially the metal ones with two pieces that you had to disconnect. On the surface, it looked impossible. There was no way anyone could separate the pieces. The pieces were metal. You couldn't bend, break, or twist them. It was what it was. I knew it could be done because the guy in the shop who sold it to me did it right in front of my eyes and then put it back together.

With that knowledge that it was possible, you had to take those two metal rods and figure it out on your own (hopefully without looking at the instructions first).

My father taught me that you can create possibilities in your life, and all you need is the willingness to be open to what's possible. You don't even have to have it all figured out. You don't need to know how you're going to do things or how they will unfold. You simply need to say yes and approach each situation with a curious mind, as if it's a puzzle or an opportunity to overcome.

That's where it all begins—with that mindset. From there, you can build on it with strategies, plans, and implementation. But without the sense of possibility, you can't create anything. You must be open to creating possibilities in your life. You have to be willing to dream and envision what you want. That step must come first before anything else can happen. You need to expand your belief system beyond what has served you in the past and into what will serve you going forward—what will help you achieve your greatness.

5-MINUTE REFLECTION:
FINDING OPPORTUNITIES TO SAY "YES"

1. Set your timer for five minutes and connect with your vision.
2. Now, scan your life for hidden opportunities to say "Yes" that support your vision.
3. Look for areas where you might have said "no" purely out of fear.
4. List three things you can say "Yes" to today.

Packing for Your Trip

WHAT'S IN YOUR SUITCASE?

Have you ever seen someone doing all the "right things," but somehow, they still don't get the job offer, finish the project, get the promotion, or lose the weight? Or there's "that person" that you try to avoid because they are always complaining, playing the victim card, constantly defensive, and everything is always someone else's fault? Or someone who has so much money and yet is still constantly complaining, unhappy, and insatiable?

And then, on the opposite extreme, you've known people who live frugally and are happy, content, grateful for what they have, and always with a smile on their face. You find yourself wanting to be around them so that their positive energy can rub off on you. What makes these two types of cases different? Mindset.

It's not what happens to us that determines our happiness or lack thereof, or the amount of money in our bank account that determines our success. Of course, there are people who get "lucky" and have a windfall of success and/or wealth without the proper mindset, but what usually happens in these cases is that their success or fortune is short-lived. So how do you start to shift your mindset?

DITCH THE EXCUSES AND DIG INTO THE COMPLAINTS

We have to identify and name the "problem" before we can transform the situation. Instead of doing that, human beings tend to come up with one of two things—**excuses** or **complaints**—and then create solutions that reduce neither.

Excuses keep you stuck in the past and unable to move forward. **Complaints** create noise and mainly suffering, which will distract you from the core problem. The great thing about complaints is that they can usually help you get closer to the problem if you know where to look. That's why you want to document the complaints. In the business setting, it's often called a **Stakeholder Interview**, but in your personal life, I'm giving you permission to have your own "**Pity Party.**"

Many women, especially women like me, have been taught to suppress our feelings. We've been called b*tchy, outspoken, too emotional, too vocal, too passionate, too [fill in the blank]. And then we wonder why we're so tired, exhausted, burnt out, depressed, and resigned. And we also wonder why we aren't able to transform the situations in our lives.

Well, I'm here to give you permission to feel. You have permission to listen to your own complaints. They are valid. Our feelings are our sensors, letting us know when we're off course from our values. Sometimes, we've lost our North Star and need to find our way back to it. Other times, we know where it is but can't see through the pain and suffering that we're causing ourselves in a particular situation. The feeling is a symptom of the "problem," shining a light on places where you need to go deeper. The deeper, the more impactful, or the harder the situation, the more layers of feelings and stories you're probably going to have to go through before you can really identify the source. And that's totally okay.

Many times, we make a situation more complex than it really is by focusing on the story rather than focusing on the vision that we want to create. It's like taking Advil for the pain but never addressing the root cause. Sure, you can keep doing that, but ultimately, you will face larger impacts and still have to address the underlying issue at some point. In either case, the needle is in that haystack of emotions, complaints, and stories we've built up around the situation. All you need to do is take out your journal and fill two pages (front and back) with unfiltered "b*tching." Pour it onto the page, feelings and all.

Consider Sarah's work situation: Sarah has a new boss that she doesn't get along with, has lost her joy, and feels like her experience and expertise aren't being utilized. The following is an excerpt from the pity party she held for herself to address the situation:

I hate work. I can't stand my new boss and his micromanaging. Why can't he trust me to do my job? I've been here five years. I am a senior resource, and he still questions what time I come in, criticizes me for the work I do, and badmouths me to the team. I don't even enjoy what I do anymore. I used to be excited to come to work, and now I just feel dread. I feel so overwhelmed and exhausted and unvalued. My experience and expertise are not even being leveraged. I know I should leave, but I have a family to support. Plus, I'm scared of starting over. I could just quit. But where would I even start? Also, how can I leave when I've put so much of my time, blood, sweat, and tears into this company? I don't want to throw away all the results I've produced. I don't know what to do.

Okay, so now you know Sarah's struggling. There's a lot to unpack there. But this is what happens when life's challenges are presented to us. Our brains look and sound like that. Even in our own minds, we jump ahead to the solution within the same conversation that we think will "fix" our "problem." We need to let all of this out first and allow ourselves to release the feelings and energy around the situation before we can even begin focusing on how to transform it. Because what you resist will persist.

THE MIRROR OF LIFE

I bet you're thinking, *It's obvious! The problem is her boss! They need to fire him, and Sarah should find a place where she's truly valued!* While those might seem like solid solutions, will they really address Sarah's core needs? More often than not, we hop from job to job only to find ourselves in the same old mess. Or we leave a relationship, only to repeat the same patterns in the next one. Why is that?

Because life is a mirror that reflects your thoughts, beliefs, and values. It's simply showing you how you see the world, including your fears, insecurities, and beliefs about what you're worthy of and what you can achieve. It's so easy to slip into the victim mindset, feeling like life is happening to you—like someone said something mean, and you just have to react. But every time I found myself stuck in that mindset, my dad would remind me, "You always have a choice!" Even when faced with seemingly insurmountable challenges, you can release your old "baggage" and make room for shifting your perspective.

MAKING ROOM FOR OPPORTUNITY

What do you do when you're out of space in your suitcase, and you need to fit more clothes? Put them in anyway and then sit on the suitcase to close it? Wrong answer (in this case). While I have definitely been guilty of overpacking and having to sit—or lie—on my suitcase to close it, there's usually an impact, like hurting my back as I try to lift my suitcase into the trunk of the Uber. Wait, isn't he supposed to help me? I might rethink that tip (lol).

In all seriousness, yes, you can continue to overpack, but at some point, there starts to be an impact. Maybe it's pulling your back muscles, maybe it's having to pay the $100 extra baggage allowance, or frantically removing clothes at the airport because you're over the baggage weight limit. I have an easier way.

When I came across *The Sedona Method* by Hale Dwoskin, I had been holding onto emotions, fears, and resentment, and was paralyzed by them. The techniques in the book really helped me in my personal life to identify and release my emotional blockage and achieve greater clarity, peace, and freedom in my life. Dwoskin uses the metaphor of a tree's roots, trunk, and branches to identify how to go deeper and remove the "roots" of any given emotion. By asking the same three questions at each level, you're able to release not only the emotions at the higher level but also the underlying blockages that are standing in your way as you weather the "storms" of life and create new beginnings. You start by asking yourself three questions about your feelings after you name them all, for example, in your "B*tch Session."

CAN I let this feeling go? WILL I let this feeling go?
If so, WHEN?

Are you willing to let your attachment to your feelings go? Are you willing to release the want that is holding you back? Are you ready to turn your situation into a solution? The key is taking the complaints and flipping each one into an opportunity as if we're standing in the future and we already have what we want that would make us happy. In other words, if you could wave a magic wand, what would the situation look like?

Take Sarah's situation. She feels stuck in her job and knows she's unhappy, but how can she transform her situation into something positive that she can focus on that reflects her values and needs? The key is first to stop referring to her situation as a "problem"—you were probably wondering why I kept putting quotes around that word—because there never is actually a problem. There is something that happened or is happening, and our perception of it. Once we can separate the two, then we can create the possibility of an opportunity in the future.

When Sarah accepts that she "perceives" these negative things "happening" to her at work, she has the power to transform the situation. She has the power to shift her mindset about what is happening in her workplace by acknowledging and releasing the emotions around her current situation. She has the power to create a new vision that empowers her, using what she doesn't like as her guide.

BELIEF REVERSAL EXERCISE

1. Write down a **limiting belief** you hold ("I'm not worthy of love" or "I'm not enough").

2. Write the opposite of that belief, your **empowering belief.** Instead of "I'm not worthy of love," try "I am worthy of love."

3. Write down three to five examples of evidence that support the empowering belief. For example:

    a. "My cats love me" (maybe it's just because I feed them, but I'll take it).

    b. "I have a wonderful group of friends that love and support me."

    c. "I have a son who loves and adores me" (*adores* might be pushing it, but he loves me).

4. If you're having a hard time coming up with examples, imagine what it would be like to act "as if" you were living and embodying that empowering belief: What would it look like if you were embodying being "worthy of love"? How would you show up for yourself? For others? For your community?

Choosing Your Travel Companions

Just as you have to be wise in your choice of travel companions to ensure a smooth and fulfilling flight and trip, you must also be mindful of the people that you surround yourself with in life. The right people can motivate you, support you, and help you move toward your destination. They can also make the journey fun, easy, and joyful.

Whether your goal is to lose weight, achieve sobriety, land a new job, move to a new house, or write a book, surround yourself with your own personal cheering squad! Find existing support groups online through Meetup.com, BetterHelp, 12-step programs, or even local gyms. You can also create your own support system by joining professional chapters or groups in your industry. If you can't find any, go ahead and start your own!

When I had my son, I hosted a Brooklyn Parents meetup in my building. I'm still friends with some of those fabulous moms I met eight years ago! When I was writing this book, I reached out to my network and formed a small publishing group of fellow aspiring and seasoned authors. We supported each other and swapped ideas, providing our own unique perspectives and support.

And let's not forget the power of an accountability partner. Exercise experts and anyone who's tried to break a habit will tell you that having someone to check in with makes a world of difference. Not only do you realize you're not alone, but you also get to learn from others who've walked the path before you. They can help you dodge those pesky pitfalls!

At the end of the day, we're social creatures. It's easy to throw in the towel when you're trying to transform your life, especially when those inner voices get loud as you get closer to success. So, stay connected! Seek out your tribe and be a support system for others, too. It'll make your journey smoother and way more fun!

CURRENT & FUTURE "CIRCLE OF SUPPORT" EXERCISE

1. Draw a circle in your notebook and divide it into four sections: Emotional Support, Practical Advice/Resources, Accountability, and Motivational Support.

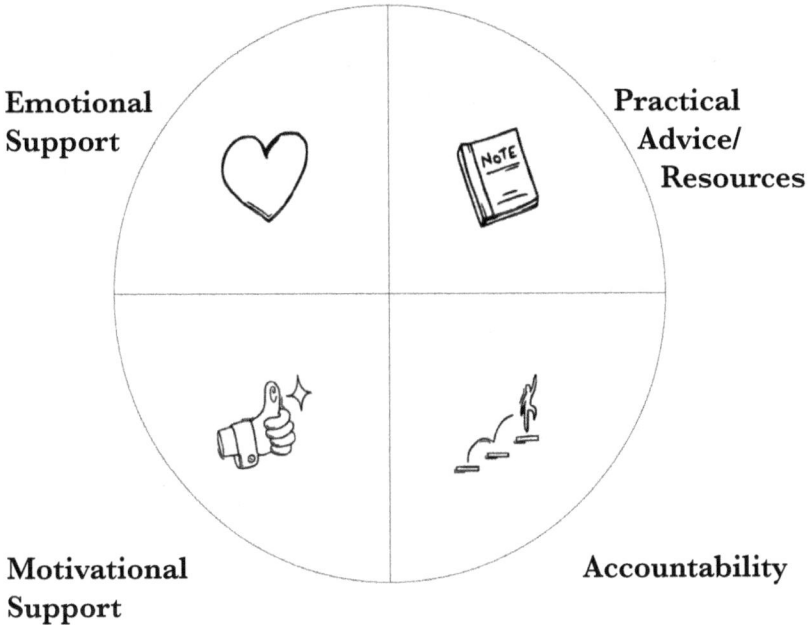

Emotional Support

Practical Advice/Resources

Motivational Support

Accountability

2. In each section, write down the names of people in your current network that provide that type of support and their relationship to you. For example, maybe your mentor might provide practical/tactical advice, or your personal trainer might provide accountability.

3. Look at each of the four sections:
   • Which sections are fully covered?
   • In which sections do you find support low or missing?
   • Are there certain people/relationships that appear in multiple sections?

4. Lastly, think about your future vision:
  - Review your current "circle of support" and the people in your current network that support you.
  - Are there any types of support needed to get to your destination that you are missing?
  - Are there people in your existing network that can provide that support?
  - If not, how can you create that support for yourself? For example, do you need to join or create a new group of supporters or strengthen any existing relationships?

Renewing Your Passport

Before you take your trip, you need to check your passport and make sure it's current. You need to find it, hold it in your hand, check its expiration date, and ensure that it has enough pages in it to travel for the next six months.

If it's outdated, you may not even be able to book your flight. However, if it's close to expiring or doesn't have enough pages for your flight, you may be turned away at the airport and need to rebook your flight. Not only does this document represent your ability to take on the journey, but it's also a tangible, living, and breathing document.

Just like you need to ensure that your passport or ID is valid so that you're able to start your new journey, you need to continually assess your skills and ensure that they are up to date. Whether that's a certification, license, degree, course, or diploma, you might be limited as you take on larger and larger goals in life without having the necessary outward "qualifications." In other cases, you might have the experience but lack the confidence to thrive in a space where others have the necessary documentation of their skillsets.

That said, don't underestimate the power of being open and willing to learn new skills. In almost every situation where you are saying "yes" to a new opportunity or goal, you will feel and/or know there's a gap between the skills you have and the skills you need. That's a sign that you're stepping out of your comfort zone and growing. It's perfectly fine to be transparent and say, "I don't have that skill yet, but I'm a quick learner and am confident that I can get up to speed quickly."

SKILLS AND QUALIFICATIONS ASSESSMENT EXERCISE

Step 1: Define Your Goal
- Think about what you want to achieve. Write it down in simple terms so it's clear.
  - *Example: "Start my own business" or "Get promoted to manager."*

Step 2: Find Out What's Needed
- What qualifications or skills are required for your goal? Do some research or ask people in similar roles. Look for things like certifications, licenses, degrees, or specific skills.
  - *Example: To be a project manager, you might need a PMP certification or experience managing teams.*

Step 3: Look at What You Already Have
- Make a list of your current skills, experiences, and qualifications that match your goal.
- What do you already bring to the table?
- What are your strengths?
  - *Example: You might already have years of leadership experience, even if you don't have a certification yet.*

Step 4: Spot the Gaps
- Compare what you need with what you have. Where are the gaps?
  - *Example: "I've managed teams before, but I don't have a formal management certification."*

Step 5: Make a Plan to Fill the Gaps

- Write down specific steps you can take to gain the missing qualifications or skills. Think about taking a course, earning a certification, or getting hands-on experience.
  - *Example: If you're missing a certification, research how to enroll in a program and plan when to start.*

Step 6: Use What You Already Have

- Don't let the gaps stop you! Highlight your existing skills and experiences while you work on building more. Confidence comes from owning what you've already accomplished.
- Remember! Once you gain a skill, that's a part of your toolbox, even if you're using it in a different setting, field, or position.
  - *Example: Your leadership skills can make you a great fit for a management role, even if you're still getting certified.*

Checking In for Your Flight

When you check in for your flight, you confirm that this goal is still important and that you're committed. You confirm that this is a goal that you still want to achieve and that the deadline is still achievable. You confirm your intention and readiness to start the journey. What is most powerful about this step is that it is the last step on your journey that you perform before launching into action, before heading to the airport, walking to your gate, or taking flight. However, this action serves as the "kick-off" of your goal: the moment that you confirm your intention and goals with the world. This is the moment the trip becomes "real."

Let's be straight with ourselves: We will all have thousands of goals in our lifetime, some of which will come to fruition and some of which won't. That's why it's important to ensure that the goals we're focusing our time and attention on are truly serving our highest good and that they are serving us as the people we are today, not outdated goals from values that we have shed along the way.

CASE IN POINT

I'm a recovering workaholic. To be honest, I've always been a workaholic. Since a young age, I thrived when I was my busiest. In college, I was a three-sport athlete, started a university magazine, and was on the Dean's list. When I got older, that translated into me traveling for work and working nights and weekends, all while trying to balance the challenges of being a mom.

Within the last year or two, my values have shifted, and I've come to value quality of life, tranquility, and downtime. If my younger self could have heard these words, she would have thought I was an imposter. That said, it's natural to review your purpose and goals continually throughout your life. By checking in with yourself and sitting in silence before embarking on any new goal, you can ensure that you're operating in complete alignment with your higher self.

Here is an exercise that can help you to verify that you're on the right track before you undertake any new goal:

5-MINUTE REFLECTION: WHY? WHY NOW?

Set your timer for five minutes and complete the following journaling exercises:

1. Go back to your list of smart goals from the previous chapter.
2. For each goal, reflect on the following questions:
   • Why is this goal important to you?
• Why is this goal important to you **right now?**
• Think of the timing of this goal. Is this the right **season** in your life to achieve this goal, or can it wait? Are there other more pressing goals?
• Check in with your body. How do you **feel** when you think of this goal? Are you living in alignment with your vision?

Flight Tip: "*The positive sign is that you feel passion and aliveness when your life is based on your vision. The negative sign is that your life feels off-course, inauthentic, and depleting when you are disconnected from your authentic vision.*"

– Dr. Jeffrey Rubin

---

3. When you buy your ticket, you choose what class you want to fly (first class, economy), which represents your level of commitment. The higher the class, the more money you're willing to invest to ensure a better experience on your journey.
   • On a scale of 1 to 10 (with 1 being the lowest and 10 being the highest), ask yourself: *How committed and motivated am I to completing this goal?*

- Is there anything that could get in the way of my accomplishing my goal?
- What can I do daily to keep me motivated?
- Who can I enlist from my support system to help me stay committed and/or hold me accountable?

Changing Your Flight

What happens if you go to check in for your flight and you realize that you overlooked a critical appointment that you have to be home for? What if you realize that this is not the right season for the trip or that this is not the goal you initially wanted? What if you've paid money and booked the flight, and then you get COVID?

Hopefully, you paid a little extra for the travel insurance, but sometimes you have to lose the money and cancel the flight altogether. Other times, you'll need to reschedule the flight or change the airline. Sometimes, you have already arrived at the airport, and you have to make this change at the gate. Other times, unexpected situations arise (aka "weather" happens), or in a real-life example, there is no pilot to fly the plane. Life happens. And that's okay.

YOU HAVE THE POWER TO CHANGE YOUR "FLIGHT"

I'm not saying this in some hokey-pokey way—I promise! In the same way that you have a choice to change your flight, you truly have the power to transform any situation you find yourself in. I know it might not feel like it right now. It can seem insurmountable, as if there's no way out of that job you loathe, that dead-end relationship, or those extra pounds. But guess what? You can get back in shape, go back to school, make new friends, discover a new hobby, or even carve out "me time" as a single or divorced mom. Want to write that book? Totally doable! (Trust me: If I can do it, you can, too!)

Deep within you lies an invincible, awe-inspiring power just waiting to be unleashed. It may be buried under all that clutter we accumulate over the years, but it's still there! You're still that gorgeous person you used to see in the mirror. It's not your reflection that's the problem; it's the grungy, plexiglass mirror you're using. And let's not even talk about those brown-tinted glasses you've been wearing! Nothing has truly changed. That amazing YOU is still waiting for the rest of you to catch up.

Whether it's changing jobs, navigating a relationship where you feel stuck, or even reassessing a friendship, it's important to remember that just because you've made a choice in the past doesn't mean you have to stick with it in the present. People grow, and sometimes we grow apart or head in different directions. The beauty of life is that you can keep choosing! Change your flight! Think of yourself as an at-will pilot in your own life—your decisions are yours to make, not by accident but by design. If you choose to stay in a friendship or relationship, that's totally valid. And if that other person decides to explore new horizons, that's perfectly okay, too! Flight canceled!

You have the agency to change your mind and make different choices, no matter how many times you've picked the same option before. If nobody's given you that permission yet, consider this your official stamp of approval!

How you handle your choices reflects your values and helps shape your character. If something isn't working for you, it's time to change it. I took this for granted until I became an adult. I remember chatting with one of my friends at a barbecue about a job where I felt disempowered, saying, "I'm not going to play the victim; I'm going to take charge of my own happiness." They looked at me like I had three heads!

I said, "Of course, I can change my mind. If I'm not feeling valued at work, I'll just leave and start my own company." One friend said, "Wait, you mean I don't have to stay at a job just because they hired me?" Exactly! If you're unhappy, you can leave. It doesn't matter if you've been there a few months; you're not chained to that job. Why suffer for someone else's gain? At the end of the day, companies are there to make money and look out for their own interests. So put yourself first and prioritize your well-being! When I told my friend this, her eyes lit up. "You're right! I didn't even think that was possible!" And there you have it: sometimes all it takes is a little reminder that you have the power to choose your own path!

Flight Tip: Transform "Have to" into "Choose to"

Do you ever hear yourself saying, "I *have to*" go to the gym, or "I *have to*" make a salad, or "I *have to* go to work"? Whenever you notice yourself saying, "I *have to*" replace it with "I *choose to*" and see how you feel. There's power in being able to choose to perform the same action but changing the language around that action. You might even find that you encounter less resistance!

Stepping Outside Your Comfort Zone

Okay, so you know you want something to change, but are you ready to climb out of that cozy little ditch? Sure, it's dark, cold, and lonely, but hey, it's familiar. Better the devil you know, as they always say! Overcoming the fear of the unknown means leaving your house, getting into that Uber, and heading to the airport.

But let's be honest: Humans love their comfort zones. Even if it's painful, we often cling to what we know despite feeling deep down that we deserve better. Yes, we're wired this way, but that doesn't mean we have to let it define us. We can override our programming, face the discomfort, and make a choice to head towards our future. But let's face it—many of us want the solution without doing the work. We shy away from taking responsibility for how we got into our situations and forget that we hold the power to get ourselves unstuck.

When I hit rock bottom (the first time) in my twenties, I felt completely lost, drowning in debt, heartbroken, and struggling with family relationships. It was a dark time, and I was severely depressed, wondering how I'd ever make it to the other side. But I had to experience that chapter in my life to get to the point where I was just so fed up—sick of being angry, exhausted, and resentful—that I was finally ready to take control of my life. It really was that simple: I made a decision. I told myself, *Enough is enough! I'm done feeling miserable!*

Now, it wasn't a full-fledged plan yet, just a commitment to change my life for the better. I stopped playing the victim and took charge of what I didn't like about my life. That decision was my turning point, much like my dad's choice to bring my brother and me to the U.S., which expanded our possibilities. I realized I had to move from relying on my dad's worldview to creating my own.

So, I took a leap of faith. I left my comfort zone and moved forward toward my vision. I didn't know how it would happen, but I decided to stay open to whatever came next. I remember sitting in my backyard in Washington, DC, coffee in hand, praying and asking God to show me the way. I said, "I don't know what's gonna happen, but I'm here, and I'm open. I know I was put on this Earth for a reason!" And that decision changed my life.

Within three months, I went from rock bottom to gazing out at my Brooklyn apartment window with a new job, money in the bank, and a renewed zest for life. It was incredibly rewarding and changed the trajectory of my adult years.

So, when I hit rock bottom (again) six years ago, I knew how to turn things around. I knew that I had done it before, from an even darker place. But that knowing didn't make it any easier. This time was different. There was more at stake. I had a little human that was depending on me now. I had to be intentional about my decisions and keep him in the forefront of all of my plans. Not only that, I was so beyond exhausted, running on empty, with only anger and determination as my fuel.

So, after my three-week pity party, full of angry rants in my journal and sobbing in the bathroom after my son was asleep, I was determined to turn things around. I returned to journaling about my purpose, my values, and my new goals. Not surprisingly, they had all changed from when I was in my twenties. I realized that I needed to rediscover who I had become, how my father's death and my marriage had shaped me, what I had learned, and what I had lost. The end of my marriage had shaken my confidence not only in relationships, but also in feelings of worth.

Even though I knew I deserved wealth and prosperity, I realized that I needed to rebuild my mindset from the ground up. I was spiraling in shame, fear, anger, and self-doubt. So, I started journaling every day to bring all of the subconscious fears to the surface and create a higher vibration of prosperity, joy, and abundance. I used affirmations, books, therapy, and personal development classes to course-correct the years of negative self-talk.

For me, it wasn't just about money. It was about living abundantly—having plenty of laughter, peace, and joyful experiences with family and friends. I wanted to operate from a place of possibility rather than limitation. It didn't matter what mistakes I had made in the past; I wasn't defined by that.

Instead, I worked on shifting my mindset and creating an empowering vision of the future that would fuel my goals and give me the motivation to achieve them. This would become the foundation that would support me as I started to take action, and that would lift me up as I encountered obstacles.

Summary

If you want to be successful in life, it's important to create a solid foundation and prepare for the journey ahead. It's about creating and acting with intention. Just as every detail matters, the work that you do to prepare for your flight will help to ensure that you arrive at your destination successfully and most importantly, with joy and fulfillment. Before you arrive at the airport and begin executing on your vision, let's make sure you've packed everything you need!

TRAVEL CHECKLIST
- ***Defined Purpose:*** *Are you clear on your purpose? How will you be of service in this lifetime? What is the legacy you want to leave behind?*
- ***Aligned Values:*** *Are you clear on your values that will create meaning and fulfillment in your life? Are they aligned with your purpose? Where are you not yet aligned?*
- ***Clear Destination:*** *Have you created a vision for your life / big-picture goals that are aligned with your values? Is the vision clear? Does it uplift you and make you excited for the future?*
- ***Ticket Purchase:*** *Have you said "Yes" to the opportunity? Have you committed to your goal?*
- ***Travel Companions:*** *What support systems do you have, or will you put in place, to support you along your journey?*
- ***Carry-On:*** *Are you packed? Were you able to shed outdated beliefs/relationships that no longer serve you and/or inhibit your achievement of future goals?*
- ***Itinerary:*** *Have you split your goals into milestones/objectives that break down your goals into smaller, more manageable pieces?*

- ***Current Passport:*** *Have you renewed or upleveled your skills/ qualifications and taken into account all of the prerequisites that are needed to allow you to begin your journey?*
- ***Check-in:*** *Have you taken time to sit quietly and consider the timing, impact, and prioritization of this particular goal within the context of your current life?*

Great! If you've just checked off all of the items in the checklist above (yes, I know it's a lot), you are ready to embark on your journey. Now, let's call that Uber and head to the airport!

Part 2:
Navigating the Airport

Welcome to the airport, where excitement meets chaos and dreams meet TSA lines. I'm your trusted flight companion, here to help you navigate this journey and ensure a smooth takeoff toward your dreams. Consider me your personal travel guide, minus the Hawaiian shirt and overly enthusiastic hand gestures.

First stop: we'll check your "passport and ticket." Do you have the essentials—skills, resources, and maybe a bit of caffeine? Next, we'll tackle your luggage. Any limiting beliefs you've been schlepping around? Let's ditch those at check-in. No need to lug around baggage that doesn't serve you. TSA (Totally Smarter Ambitions) would disapprove. Security's up next—time to face those pesky obstacles and come up with a plan to breeze through them like a pro. With your "boarding pass" (aka SMART goals) in hand, we'll break those goals into bite-sized steps, like finding your gate without stopping for overpriced snacks. Ok, fine, maaaaaybe we'll stop if we have time. I'll show you how to prioritize all of the options you have in front of you so that you're set up for success.

Once we board, you'll step into your power and find your "seat." You'll assess your strengths, own your role, and commit to the journey. As we taxi, we'll review the "safety card"—what's your Plan B if Plan A hits turbulence? And finally, as the plane takes off, we'll confront the big one: fear of flying. Failure? Success? Reframe them both into fuel for your journey!

Ticket & Passport Check

You arrive at the airport, ideally two to three hours ahead of your scheduled international flight, and have plenty of time. But does that matter if you've forgotten your passport and/or cannot find/print your boarding pass?

Every goal has a series of prerequisites—skills, information, and/or resources required to achieve it. Before you can even print out your boarding pass, someone at the ticket counter has to confirm that you have your essential items for your flight—your ID and ticket for your particular trip. By incorporating this preliminary step into your goal, you can gather the essentials to avoid setbacks and set yourself up for success.

So, how do you identify the prerequisites for your unique goal? Start by thinking about what could derail your goal from getting to the starting point. For example, if your goal is to run a marathon, the prerequisites might include what is required to "qualify" to enter the race (completed a certain number of qualifying races and/or achieved a specific qualifying time in previous races).

Knowing the prerequisites of a particular goal allows you to prepare and take those initial steps to ultimately board your plane. It may seem overwhelming, but it doesn't have to be. Think about what you need to do before you can board the plane. You've already completed some of those steps at home (booking the flight, packing, checking in) and arrived at the airport. Now you have to present your passport and go through security, to the right terminal, and then to the correct gate. Those are just objectives or "milestones" along the way to ensure you have a fighting shot at getting on the plane!

For the marathon example, a sample prerequisite list might look like this:

If I want to register for the 2026 Boston Marathon, I first need to:

1. **Qualify for the Marathon.**
   - To qualify for the Boston Marathon, I must first finish a qualified marathon at least three minutes faster than the qualifying time for my gender and age group.
     - *To do that,* I need to know the qualifying time for my gender and age group.
     - AND I also need to know what a qualifying marathon is.
       - *To do that,* I need to review the approved qualifying marathons.
     - AND I need to run the qualified marathon three minutes faster than the qualifying time.
       - *To do that,* I need to create a training plan that prepares me to run three minutes faster than the qualifying team.

2. **Register by the deadline.**
   - To register by the deadline, I have to receive a reminder in my calendar.
     - *To do that,* I must have added the date with a reminder to my calendar.
       - *To do that,* I must have created or purchased a calendar.

3. **Pay the registration fee of $250.**
   - To pay the registration fee, I have to save $250.
     - *To do that,* I need to reduce my spending in another area of my budget.
       - *To do that,* I need to know what I'm spending.
         - *To do that,* I need to create a monthly budget.

Now it's your turn!

PREREQUISITES ASSESSMENT EXERCISE

With the insights that you've gotten from the last two exercises, write down as many purpose statements as you can for each of the following four quadrants.

1. For each of your objectives, list the prerequisites (skills, activities, qualifications, resources) before you can even register or commit to your goal. In the case of the marathon example, if one of the prerequisites is completing a certain number of qualifying races, then you would list out each qualifying event.

2. Then, continue to work backward from the ultimate goal. What actions must occur to complete each qualifying event? This might mean completing the 10k within the qualifying time for your age group, running the 10k, registering for the 10k, purchasing a pair of running shoes, etc.

3. Next, you need to identify gaps that need your attention so you can prioritize your time. For each prerequisite action, rank your current level of completion on a scale of 1 to 5 (1 being totally **unprepared** and 5 being fully **prepared**).

4. For the items with a ranking lower than a 5, estimate how much time it will take for you to complete that action item.

5. Now, review the action items. Prioritize the most time-intensive tasks. Are there actions you can perform simultaneously/in parallel?

6. Lastly, set a deadline for each task, assuming you could start the most time-intensive task tomorrow and complete each task sequentially.

7. Lastly, add all of these deadlines into a simple project management tool like Monday.com, an Excel sheet, calendar, or even a piece of paper as a checklist that you can track.

High-Altitude Hack: I prefer to use an online project management tool like Monday.com or Smartsheet.com to manage prerequisites. A tool like that can automatically spit out new dates for your prerequisites if one date slips or a deadline changes. Otherwise, you have to manually go in and cross out the original dates.

Checking Your Luggage

If you've brought more than a carry-on for your flight, you'll need to check your bags and pick them up at your destination. Why is that? Having them on the plane will make the plane too heavy to fly and possibly cause you to crash before you reach your destination.

You might be wondering why you need to revisit your belief system. "Didn't I just do this when I packed my suitcase?" I hear you say. Well, some beliefs are in your "blind spot," and you're unable to see how much they're slowing you down when you're initially preparing for your goal. You know they're "heavy," but you're willing to carry them, even if your back is hurting from lifting them into and out of the car. And they don't show themselves until you start taking action toward your goal, confronting that belief through action.

You know that they're there, but sometimes, you need a special scale to see them clearly so that you can remove them and continue on your journey. If there are beliefs that are weighing you down too heavily, you need to set them aside and suspend them until you complete your goal, if not forever.

The bigger the goal, the more you can expect limiting beliefs to rear their ugly heads. It's their job to "protect you" and keep you "safe," and they will be threatened when you're leaping into the unknown.

So, set your timer for five minutes. Let's weigh your suitcase and see if there are any beliefs that are weighing you down.

**5-MINUTE REFLECTION:
EXAMINING YOUR LIMITING BELIEFS**

1. Write down five limiting beliefs that come up for you as you start to get into action.
2. For each belief, ask yourself:
   • Where did it come from?
• Something happened, and you made up a belief about life, yourself, or other people. Do you remember the source?
• Is this belief *still* serving you?

   We create beliefs throughout our lives, and they serve us in some way, up to a point. If we look at our beliefs and challenge them, we will sometimes see that a long-held belief stopped serving us a long time ago. This belief may have kept you safe from real or perceived danger.
• What is the cost of holding on to this belief?
• Is this belief costing you peace, relationships, joy, or wealth? What impact has this belief had on your life?
• What would life look like without this belief?
• Imagine being freed from this belief. What opportunities would be available to you? How would you feel?
• How can you replace this belief with one that empowers you?

High-Altitude Hack: If you need an example, refer to the "Belief Reversal Exercise" in the "Packing for Your Trip" chapter.

Security Check

Okay, you've checked your luggage, shown your passport and boarding pass, and gotten to the security scanners.

Is there anything you're carrying that might get in the way or pose a risk on your flight? Did you forget to throw out or empty your water bottle? Did you accidentally pack something sharp or dangerous? Did you knowingly or unknowingly exceed your 3-ounce allowance of fluids?

This is an opportunity to check for any obstacles that might hinder your ability to achieve your goals. By anticipating these, you can put a strategy in place to anticipate and mitigate those obstacles before they occur.

One of the biggest obstacles that we put in our own path is comparing ourselves to others. Competing with others is like chasing your own tail. You might notice someone with more skills, but remember, there will always be someone "better" and "worse" than you in any field. Instead, focus on leveling up your own game. After all, who knows you better than you?

I get it. It's human nature to want to win and be competitive. We all want to be the best version of ourselves! But here's the thing: competing against others only adds unnecessary pressure. It can make you feel small and even cause you to shut down when things get tough.

So, ditch that mindset. The only person you need to compete against is yourself. Let go of the comparisons and the "They're doing better than me" noise in your mind. Sometimes, it's easy to forget that much of what we see isn't even real, especially on social media!

Let's be honest: Competing against an idealized version of someone else is like trying to hit a moving target. Instead, ask yourself, *How can I get better? What can I learn? How can I perfect my craft?* Embrace that journey, and you'll empower yourself to grow and expand your possibilities.

Remember, it's all about you and your progress! So, let's review some of the additional obstacles that you might run into and see how we can prevent them from happening:

OBSTACLES ASSESSMENT EXERCISE

1. Complete the following assessment, ranking each obstacle on a scale of 1 to 10 in terms of its impact on your goal's success.

Category	Potential Obstacle	Impact	Scale (1-10)
External Factors	Resources	Limited access to necessary resources, such as finances, technology, tools, or external support, can limit or stop your progress.	
	Unsupportive Environment	A lack of support from family, friends, and/or co-workers can make it more difficult to stay motivated and lead you to feel isolated.	
	Unexpected Life Events	Personal emergencies, health issues or personal/professional demands can derail your plans and require extra commitment and resilience to get you back on track.	
	Competitive or Market Changes	In your professional/business-related goals, economic downturns, increased competition, and shifting market trends can create unexpected challenges.	

Category	Potential Obstacle	Impact	Scale (1-10)
Planning & Execution	Unclear or Unambitious Goals	When your goals are too vague or lack a spark of ambition, it's like setting off on a trip with no map or destination—you'll wander aimlessly and lose momentum. Without clear, measurable objectives to guide you, it's easy to lose focus, stall out, or even forget why you started in the first place.	
	Lack of Planning/ Structure	Without a clear timeline or roadmap, it's difficult to track your progress and stay organized, leading to missed goals and/or steps.	
	Failure to Create Milestones	Skipping small, achievable checkpoints makes it harder to gauge your progress and adjust your plan as needed.	
	Resistance/ Inflexibility to Change	Rigidity in your approach can make it difficult to adapt to shifting circumstances, and being unwilling to pivot or adjust your goal might limit success.	
	Procrastination & Poor Time Management	Delaying action can cause small tasks to pile up.	

Category	Potential Obstacle	Impact	Scale (1-10)
Emotional/ Psychological Barriers	Burnout/Stress	Overworking or lacking balance can lead to mental and/or physical exhaustion, making it difficult to focus and perform at your peak.	
	Perfectionism	Holding yourself to an unrealistic standard can cause you to overthink, make you fearful of taking any action, or cause you to procrastinate.	
	Comparing Yourself with Other People	Constantly measuring yourself against other people can make you feel discouraged and/or jealous and prevent you from being motivated to achieve your goals.	

2. Are there obstacles you can prevent from occurring altogether? How? What actions do you need to take to prevent them? What support do you need?

Reviewing Your Boarding Pass

Whether you get a boarding pass printed out at the ticket counter/airport kiosk or pull it up on your phone, you need to have documentation that you are authorized to board your particular flight on the way to your exact destination. Even though you already cleared initial security, airport personnel continue to check and verify your information, even at the gate, prior to boarding.

Why is this important? Because—believe it or not—some people still try to sneak onto planes, and many others board the wrong flights by mistake. Or maybe they get on the right flight and end up sitting in the wrong seats. Other times, people miss their flight because they weren't aware of the boarding time (and forgot that the doors close 15–30 minutes before takeoff). Even I've learned the hard way, having the airplane doors close on me as I ran down the corridor! It's hard enough making the flight *with* a boarding pass, let alone without one.

Another thing that you'll notice on a boarding pass is that the most urgent information (the departure information) is listed twice, once on the main part of the boarding pass and another on a smaller column that the gate personnel can tear off when you're boarding. This re-emphasizes the importance of taking those initial steps to arrive on the plane.

Arrival: This section describes our destination, including the airport, city, and arrival deadline (day and time). Interestingly enough, this is the shortest section of the boarding pass.

The rest of the boarding pass includes the objectives (or steps) we must complete before our goal takes off!

- **TSA Pre-Check:** Your positive mindset and belief system have earned you the trust of yourself and others, which means you're cleared to go through expedited security.
- **Departure:** This section describes our starting point, a guide for getting to our plane (Terminal and Gate), plus two

important deadlines for starting our journey: the boarding time and the departure time.

- **Departure Airport > Terminal > Gate > Plane**
  - Even if you've already arrived at the right airport, you still need to find your way to the plane. To do that, you have to start general and get more specific. For example, you have to take the necessary steps (or shuttle) to arrive at the correct terminal. Once you're in the right terminal, your next task is to find your specific gate. Even after you've arrived at your gate, you still have to listen for the boarding announcement, get in line and board the plane.
  - Once you're on the plane, you have to take off, reach cruising altitude, descend, and land the plane. This is analogous to breaking our goals down into smaller outcomes or objectives.
  - This is a critical part of goal-setting: to break down a large goal or project into manageable parts, and use markers to give you milestones along the way.
- **Boarding time**
  - Your boarding time is your deadline to get on the plane before the plane doors close. In essence, missing your boarding time can prevent you from catching the flight, making it a "prerequisite" or something required before you can even start your journey.
  - Our set of "prerequisites" is everything we need to complete to achieve our final goal.
- **Flight #:** This is the specific plane and path that will take us on the journey, including the space that we are holding for that goal to take shape. This flight correlates to the specific flight plan that our plane will use to get to our destination. This is also the path that we are choosing to be on vs. another path to another destination. In the overarching metaphorical scheme we are using here, this represents prioritizing this goal as important and meaningful for you to participate in now.

- **Seat Assignment:**
  - Your seat assignment shows your individual place on the plane. In some cases, you'll be a solo traveler sitting in the pilot's seat, and in other cases (like a marriage), you'll be sitting in the co-pilot's seat. Sometimes, you'll be flying on a commercial flight where you'll have an assigned seat, and someone else is flying the plane. In all three scenarios, your seat represents your personal responsibility toward achieving your particular goal.
  - The seat you're located in designates your involvement in the journey. In many cases, as you're embarking on new journeys in life, there will be many goals where you're not actually doing the work. You may be accountable for getting it done, like air traffic control or the pilot, who is directly responsible for getting the plane to the destination safely. Or you could be the person who is advising. It's vital to be clear on your roles and responsibilities and how you and anyone else involved in the journey will contribute to success. This is especially crucial when taking on career goals where you depend on a team.

TRANSFORMING YOUR VISION INTO A SERIES OF SMART GOALS

As mentioned previously, a SMART goal is characterized by the following qualities:
- **S**pecific: has a clearly defined outcome.
- **M**easurable: Can be tracked and measured.
- **A**chievable: This is something that you can realistically achieve with your given resources and time *and* is aligned with the values that govern your life.
- **R**elevant: Fits into your vision and long-term strategy.
- **T**ime-bound: Has a deadline/timeframe for when it will be completed.

When I've had a vision in my life that I wanted to achieve, I've first transformed the vision into a series of SMART goals, building in the values and needs that were important to me. Consider my goal of moving to New York. I had created the vision. I was clear on what I wanted. To make that a reality, I had to transform my vision into clear, measurable goals.

The next step was to create two to three SMART goals. Here are two of the ones I created:

1. **I will accept a job offer in NYC by Sept 30th for 25 percent more than my current salary from a company that aligns with my values and where I can leverage my project management skills.**
   a. *S - **What will I do?**: I will get a job at a NYC-based company.*
   b. *M - **How will I define success?**: I will accept a job offer with an annual salary that is 25% more than I'm making now, at a company with a culture of fun, work/life balance, where my project management skills are in demand, and which gives me the flexibility to perform in the evenings.*
   c. *A - **How will I ensure this is achievable?**: I will update my resume, LinkedIn, and resume sites, and apply to 100 project management positions in New York City.*
   d. *R - **How is this relevant to my vision?**: My day job will give me both the financial freedom and the time to perform with my band, which is very important to me.*
   e. *T - **By when will I achieve this goal?**: I will achieve this goal by Sep. 30th (three months from now).*

2. I will sign a one-year lease by Oct. 30th for a Brooklyn apartment with a monthly rent of $1000 or less.

    a. S - What will I do?: I will live in Brooklyn, NY.

    b. M - How will I define success?: I will have signed a one-year lease for a one-bedroom Brooklyn apartment in a safe neighborhood with a rent of $1000 or less.

    c. A - How will I ensure this is achievable?: I will ensure I have a job before I make the final move, and save up enough money for rent + security deposit and spending money for 2 months.

    d. R - How is this relevant to my vision?: In my vision, I am living in New York City.

    e. T - By when will I achieve this goal?: I will achieve this goal by Oct. 30th (four months from now).

SMART GOAL EXERCISE

This exercise focuses on assessing your goals using the **SMART** criteria: **Specific, Measurable, Achievable, Relevant,** and **Time-bound**. It is designed to help you develop clear and attainable goals.

Steps:

1. Write down the goal you wish to achieve.
2. Evaluate your goal against each of the components of the **SMART** framework:
   - **Specific:** Is your goal clear? Can you answer these questions: Who? What? Where? When? Why?
   - **Measurable:** How will you know if you're getting closer to your goal? Is there a way to tell when you have reached it?
   - **Achievable:** Is your goal realistic? Do you have the skills, resources, and time you need to achieve it?
   - **Relevant:** Does your goal match your bigger plans and values? Is this the right time to work on it?
   - **Time-bound:** Does your goal have a deadline? When do you want to finish it?

3. Does your goal meet all the **SMART** criteria?
   - If not, what changes can you make to ensure that your goal does meet the criterion in question?
   - Also, are there any resources you might be missing that could hold you back from reaching this goal?

This exercise helps ensure your goal is well-structured and achievable, making it more likely that you'll follow through.

Finding Your Gate

If you've followed the previous steps in the process, you're now clear on what you want. You can see the movie of how your life will look. You have your boarding pass, so you know what you want to achieve and by when. But how do you get there? It can seem so far off and unattainable. It doesn't have to be. I'm going to show you how to break your goal down into smaller sections so that you have markers along the way.

Without breaking up your goals into smaller steps and checkpoints to ensure that you arrive at your gate on time, it's very easy to miss your flight. This is why it's essential to set clear, actionable objectives to find your way to the gate, just as they are crucial to achieving personal and professional success.

First, you have to start at the end, imagining that you have achieved the result. Then, think about the major benchmarks that you have to achieve to get to that result. Now, add a deadline to each of the benchmarks. What needs to be done before that, and before that, and before that? These are the smaller sets of results that you want to have achieved and should be quantifiable, a number where possible.

What do I mean by that? It's about breaking things down into smaller, more manageable time chunks or milestones. You can slice years into quarters, quarters into months, months into weeks, and weeks into days. I know it can feel a bit overwhelming, but don't sweat it! You don't need to map out every single step right now. Trust me: this approach makes planning your personal life a breeze!

In my case, once I started working backward from October 30th (my end goal) of moving to New York, I created four monthly milestones to allow me to track my progress toward moving to New York. By adding deadlines, I could see if I was on track for my larger goal and adjust if needed.

Here is what my milestones looked like:

1. **Sign my lease.**
   a. **Deadline:** October 30th
   b. **Outcome Achieved:** Signed lease and paid deposit for a one-bedroom apartment in Brooklyn in a safe area with a monthly rent of $1000 or less.
2. **Visit ten apartments.**
   a. **Deadline:** September 30th
   b. **Outcome Achieved:** Accepted job offer and visited ten apartment open houses from among the 30 listings.
3. **Review 30 apartment listings.**
   a. **Deadline:** August 31st
   b. **Outcome Achieved:** Reviewed 30 online listings for apartments in my three neighborhoods.
4. **Research where I want to live.**
   a. **Deadline:** July 31st
   b. **Outcome Achieved:** Researched and identified three Brooklyn neighborhoods to live in that are safe areas for a single woman.

Your turn!

MILESTONES EXERCISE

This exercise is all about making those big, complex goals feel a lot more manageable by breaking them down into smaller, bite-sized milestones (important achievements or checkpoints) that move you closer to your goal.

1. **Write Down Your SMART Goal**
   a. Take one of the SMART goals that you created in the previous chapter.
2. **Break It Down into Milestones**
   a. Divide your goal into smaller, manageable milestones that represent key steps along the way.

Sample Milestones for a Simple Website:
1. Choose a website platform.
2. Choose a website template.
3. Write and add content for main pages.
4. Design and add images for main pages.
5. Update SEO (Search Engine Optimization) tags.
6. Launch the site.

3. Assign Realistic Deadlines to Each Milestone

a. Be mindful of the amount of time each step requires, alongside any other commitments you have.

For Example:
1. Choose a website platform by [Date].
2. Choose a website template by [Date].
3. Write and add content for main pages by [Date].
4. Design and add images for main pages by [Date].
5. Update SEO tags by [Date].
6. Launch the site by [Date].

4. Identify Resources and Support Needed: For each

milestone, note any resources, tools, or support you might need. This could include software, feedback from a mentor, or access to specific information. Example: "I'll need access to a web hosting provider, content examples, and design tools."

5. Schedule it!

• Create a tracking method that works for you. This could be a digital app, spreadsheet, or physical calendar. Mark off each milestone as you complete it, and note any adjustments or delays along the way.

Remember, breaking your goal into smaller milestones helps create a clear path forward and makes it all feel a lot less overwhelming. You've got this!

Prioritizing Your Time Before the Flight

Congratulations on reaching the gate! That's an exciting milestone on your journey! Now that you have some time to spare before boarding, let's make the most of it together. There's plenty you can do to pass the time, and I'm here to help you focus on what matters.

First off, let's chat about those tempting snacks you noticed on your way to the gate. Sure, that fancy bag of candy or the latest issue of People magazine might have caught your eye. But take a moment to consider if they're truly essential right now. It's easy to get distracted by celebrity gossip—trust me, if Taylor Swift and Travis Kelce have any big news, it'll be all over Instagram before you know it! Skipping those distractions lets you keep your eye on the prize—your flight! If you have lots of time to spare, then by all means, enjoy!

Now, let's talk about those little emergencies that pop up—like the kid who needs to go to the bathroom right now. It may be urgent, but in the grand scheme, it's manageable. Like a flat tire on the way to the airport—it can feel like a big deal, but it won't prevent you from taking off. Just handle it now to avoid any extra surprises on the plane—everyone will thank you for it!

Then we have the all-important lunch decision. While fueling your body is crucial, it's not necessarily urgent. You can easily grab a bite on the plane. It might not be gourmet dining (sorry, JetBlue!), but it's certainly doable. Think of it like packing your suitcase in advance—it's smart, but it isn't something you have to tackle right this minute. Oh, wait, you're one of those proactive packers? My dream is to be you when I grow up.

Then there's the final boarding call, which is both urgent and important! Getting on your plane is a top priority; it's like meeting a crucial deadline at work. You can't afford to overlook it, and it naturally rises to the top of your to-do list.

BUT WHAT IF MULTIPLE TASKS COME CRASHING IN AT ONCE?

Now, that's the real challenge! When faced with several urgent and important tasks, it's time to take stock of each one. Consider their deadlines and potential impact.

Did you accidentally leave your phone in the bathroom stall? How quickly can you retrieve it? Is it worth the risk of losing your phone compared to the potential costs of rescheduling your flight? And if you're headed to a wedding that you absolutely cannot miss, that phone becomes a distant secondary worry; someone lucky might just find an unexpected gift waiting for them!

Remember, navigating these priorities can be a bit of a maze, but some decisions are definitely tougher than others. Focus on the most important tasks first!

So, as you enjoy this time before takeoff, keep those priorities in mind. Stay clear of tempting distractions like snacks or unnecessary breaks if you're pressed for time. Fuel up on the plane, and above all, don't miss that flight! Safe travels!

EISENHOWER MATRIX EXERCISE

Ready to transform how you tackle your to-do list? The Eisenhower Matrix is a fantastic tool that helps prioritize tasks based on **urgency** and **importance**. It was inspired by Dwight D. Eisenhower, the 34th U.S. President, who famously said: "What is important is seldom urgent, and what is urgent is seldom important."

This will help you focus on what really matters most to you! Let's jump in and learn how to prioritize like a pro!

Step 1: List Your Tasks

First things first! Take a moment to jot down everything you're working on.

Here's an example to get you started:
1. *Finish the Q4 Performance Reviews for my team.*
2. *Reply to emails.*
3. *Do laundry.*
4. *Get ready for tomorrow's meeting.*
5. *Pick up (or order) groceries.*
6. *Call Aunt Joan to see how her knee surgery went.*
7. *Send out the project proposal.*
8. *Attend Friday happy hour with my fabulous mom group.*

Step 2: Categorize Your Tasks

Now, let's sort those tasks into the four quadrants of the Eisenhower Matrix:

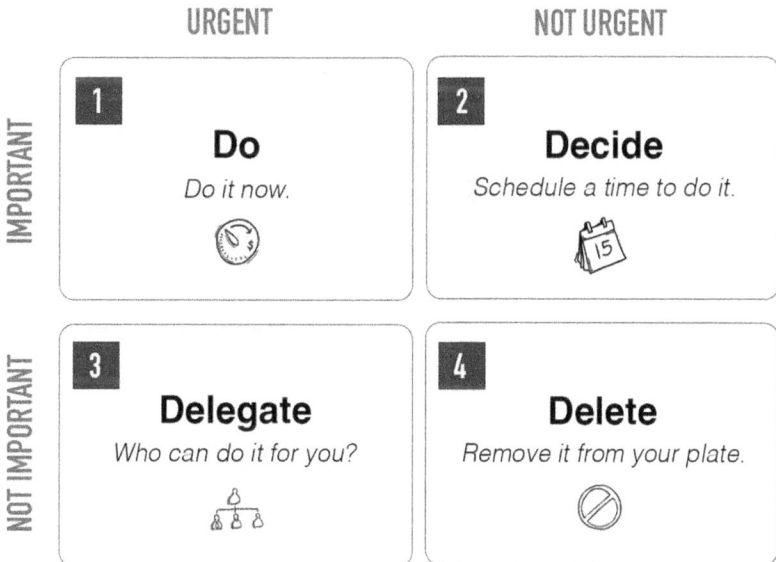

	URGENT	NOT URGENT
IMPORTANT	**1** **Do** *Do it now.*	**2** **Decide** *Schedule a time to do it.*
NOT IMPORTANT	**3** **Delegate** *Who can do it for you?*	**4** **Delete** *Remove it from your plate.*

- **Urgent and Important** *(Quadrant 1)*: These are the tasks that need your immediate attention and are super important. Do them immediately.
- **Not Urgent but Important** *(Quadrant 2)*: These tasks are key for your long-term success but don't need to be done right away. Schedule a time to do them.
- **Urgent but Not Important** *(Quadrant 3)*: These are tasks that require a quick response but won't greatly affect your long-term goals. If possible, delegate these tasks to others.
- **Not Urgent and Not Important** *(Quadrant 4)*: These tasks can be put off since they aren't time-sensitive or crucial. Either take them off your list completely or schedule a time to revisit them at the end of the week.

Example Categorization:
- *Quadrant 1 (Urgent & Important):*
  - *Finish the Q4 Performance Reviews for my team (due tomorrow).*
  - *Prepare for the meeting (tomorrow).*
- *Quadrant 2 (Not Urgent & Important):*
  - *Review the project proposal (due next week).*
  - *Do laundry (I have a few more days before this becomes urgent).*
- *Quadrant 3 (Urgent & Not Important):*
  - *Reply to emails (some need quick responses).*
  - *Call Aunt Joan to see how her knee surgery went (call her this week).*
- *Quadrant 4 (Not Urgent & Not Important):*
  - *Pick up or order groceries (can wait a few days, thank you, Seamless).*
  - *Attend Friday happy hour with my mom group (optional, not crucial... or is it??).*

Step 3: Prioritize Within Each Quadrant
- Now that you've sorted your tasks, it's time to prioritize them within each quadrant.
- Pay attention to deadlines and how important each task is. For example, start with that presentation in Quadrant 1 since it's coming up soon!

Step 4: Take Action
- Start with Quadrant 1 tasks.
- Once you've tackled those, move on to Quadrant 2. And remember, it's totally okay to delegate or put off tasks in Quadrants 3 and 4 when you can!

Step 5: Review Regularly
- Make it a habit to check your task list regularly. This way, you can evaluate any new responsibilities and prioritize them thoughtfully.

By embracing this method, you'll boost your productivity and focus on what truly matters in your life. Here's to happy prioritizing and smashing those goals! You've got this!

Finding Your Seat &
Fastening Your Seatbelt

When you board your plane, it's time to find your seat and "step into your power." This is the time to look at yourself and identify your strengths and unique contributions that will give you confidence for your goal. These will be things you can draw upon as the journey progresses, and help you figure out the key skills and qualities you want within your support system.

All of this helps you take ownership of your contribution to the outcome and your potential for success. In addition, there are various seats: the pilot, co-pilot, and then window, center, and aisle in the main section of the plane. Each of these seats has different viewpoints, challenges, and responsibilities. You will find yourself in different seats on different goals/projects.

CORE STRENGTHS EXERCISE
Here is an exercise to help you identify your strengths and understand what makes you powerful by embracing the skills you already bring to the table.

Write down your answers to the following questions:
1. What are three skills or areas that I'm naturally good at?
2. What do other people come to me for support and guidance with?
3. What accomplishments am I most proud of? What strengths helped me achieve them?
4. Set a goal to take one small action a day to reinforce your personal power. For example,

a. Share an idea or speak up in a meeting.

b. Decline a request that doesn't align with your goals or priorities.

c. Say yes to something that will push you past your comfort zone, whether it's taking a different route home, trying a new food, learning a new vocabulary word, or saying hi to someone new at work.

Watching the Safety Message

Have you noticed that every flight you board has one of those safety cards in the front seat pocket, and the flight attendants take five minutes at the beginning of every flight to go over the exit routes and evacuation procedures? They know that it's difficult, if not impossible, to create a plan when you're in a crisis and in survival mode. And as airtight as you think your plan and goals are, there is always a high chance that something won't go according to plan and a small chance that the goal will crash and burn.

As I've discovered time and time again, there are just some things in life you can't control! You can have the perfect plan, a stellar team, and a clear objective, but sometimes things go awry. When things don't go according to plan, I've had to learn to let go of the frustration. I mean, we had a budget and a deadline—how could this happen?

Two key things helped me release that need for control.

First: Reciting the Serenity Prayer and forcing myself to accept that I can't always control what happens (no matter how hard I try or will it to happen).

Serenity Prayer: *God, grant me the serenity to accept the things I cannot change, the courage to change the things I can, and the wisdom to know the difference.*

Second: Create a mitigation plan to control the "controllables"! It's like creating a backup dance for when the main act goes off-script. Before diving into a project, I brainstorm all the potential hiccups—like speakers dropping out, funding vanishing, or tech glitching out. If you know what could go wrong, it's no surprise when it happens. You can say, "Okay, if X happens, we'll do Y!"

And sure, some situations are completely out of our hands. If the event gets canceled or postponed, at least you've got a game plan for how to handle it. Knowing the protocol in advance takes the sting out of surprises and prevents the stress levels of dealing with a situation you weren't expecting.

I know that some people say you should only have a "Plan A." I've tried that approach, but in my personal and professional experience, that approach causes more frustration and disappointment than thinking through all of the options and creating a "Plan B," "Plan C," and "Plan D," based on circumstances that arise. This doesn't mean that you can't commit to "Plan A," but you get a chance to think through what will happen if things don't go according to plan. Sometimes, just going through this process upfront can also cause you to change your goal or pause it until you have done more preparation.

IF/THEN PLANNING EXERCISE

1. Identify Potential Obstacles

    a. Write down possible obstacles or situations that could make it hard to reach your goal. *Example.: If your goal is to exercise three times a week, an obstacle might be "feeling too tired after work."*

2. Create "If" Scenarios for Each Obstacle

    a. For each obstacle, start with "If…" and add the situation that could prevent you from staying on track. *Example: "If I feel too tired after work…"*

3. Define the "Then" Actions to Address Each Scenario

    a. For each "if" scenario, add a "then" statement with an action that helps you handle the obstacle. *Example: "If I feel too tired after work, then I'll do a 10-minute walk or stretch instead of a full workout."*

4. Practice and Adjust

    a. Try putting your if/then statements into action as obstacles arise. If an approach doesn't work, adjust it to make it more effective.

5. Review and Expand

    a. Add more if/then statements for different scenarios to cover a range of situations. Having a variety of if/then plans prepares you for various challenges.

Release Your Fear of "Flying"

Just like boarding an airplane, chasing new opportunities often means stepping out of our comfort zone and facing the unknown. Both experiences remind us of our desire to be comfortable while also craving the thrill that comes with growth.

As we prepare for "takeoff" in life, it's completely natural to feel a mix of excitement and nervousness. We know this journey could lead to amazing successes or a few bumps along the way. Takeoff is such an important moment; it's when doubts might feel most intense. While we sit in our seats, our minds race with thoughts about what could happen next. The roar of the plane's engines and its ascent can be compared to how our goals encourage us to reach for greater heights. During this phase, it's common for fear to appear in different forms. We might find ourselves worrying about failing or feeling anxious about what success could bring. Leaving the familiar ground can be unsettling, and facing new challenges often pushes us to confront our limits and fears regarding our dreams.

Interestingly, fear of success isn't talked about as much, but it can be just as powerful as fear of failing. We might catch ourselves thinking, *What if I succeed? Will I be able to handle it? How will it change my relationships? Will I be able to sustain it? Do I even deserve it?* This kind of fear can trap us, making us hesitate to seize new opportunities, even when they're exciting and full of promise.

As we embrace the unknown, this journey really tests our growth and resilience. That uneasy feeling during takeoff often transforms into a sense of freedom as the airplane lifts off. This change is much like how we can overcome doubts and start to believe in ourselves. If we can embrace discomfort and recognize that both success and failure are part of the adventure, we'll uncover our strengths and rise above our fears.

Ultimately, being scared to fly offers us valuable lessons that extend far beyond the airport—lessons about courage, adaptability, and self-trust. Just as pilots must trust their training when taking off, we, too, need to build our confidence as we embark on the journey toward our dreams. It's key to remember that it's perfectly okay for fear and excitement to coexist. By facing these feelings head-on, we can shift our perspective on success and failure, turning our potential into real achievements and taking flight toward our dreams!

"WHAT'S THE WORST THAT COULD HAPPEN" EXERCISE

This exercise helps you break down the underlying fears associated with your limiting beliefs and replace them with a more grounded experience.

1. Write down a limiting belief that triggers fear for you. For example, "I'll never make enough money to support myself and my family."
2. Break down the belief into the different fears that it creates.
   a. Examples: fear of failure, fear of success, fear of being judged, fear of making a mistake
3. For each fear, ask yourself:
a. Is this fear real or imaginary?
   b. What is the worst-case scenario, and how likely is it to happen?
   c. What is the best-case scenario?
   d. Which small, manageable steps can I take to address this fear and move forward?
   e. How can I reframe my belief to focus on the possibilities rather than the fear?
4. Lastly, ask yourself, "What if everything goes well?" Visualize each step, imagining what a positive outcome would look like and how you'd feel.
   a. Ask yourself:
      • What would it look like if I succeeded?
      • What steps would I take if I believed success was possible?

Summary

Congratulations on navigating the airport and getting on the plane! In this chapter, you completed the final prerequisites, allowing you to kick off the project. This process allowed you to board confidently and begin the journey toward your goal, organized and well-prepared. Let's review your Travel Checklist to ensure you have everything you need before you take off!

TRAVEL CHECKLIST

- ***ID & Ticket:*** *Do you have the essential items for your journey?*
- ***Checked Luggage:*** *Have you reviewed any new limiting beliefs that arose after you started your journey?*
- ***Cleared Security:*** *Have you assessed your potential obstacles and identified actions that might help you prevent them?*
- ***Reviewed Boarding Pass:*** *Have you created SMART goals that transform your vision into concrete results that can be tracked and achieved?*
- ***Found Your Gate:*** *Have you broken down your SMART goals into smaller steps and objectives that will allow you to kick off your goals?*
- ***Boarded the Plane:*** *Have you taken the initial steps to move out of the preparation stage and begin the execution of your goals?*
- ***Found Your Seat:*** *Have you assessed the unique strengths and contributions that you bring to the goal? Have you identified and owned your part in achieving the goal?*
- ***Reviewed the Safety Message:*** *Have you created and thought through Plans B, C, and D if Plan A should fail? Are you clear on the trade-offs and impacts of each plan?*
- ***Overcome Your Fear of Flying:*** *Lastly, have you faced your fears of failure AND success? Have you reframed that fear into a belief that empowers you?*

Now that you're in your seat and ready to fly, let's review the flight plan, create momentum, and begin tracking your goals toward completion! You're officially on your way to achieving greatness!

Part 3:
The Flight

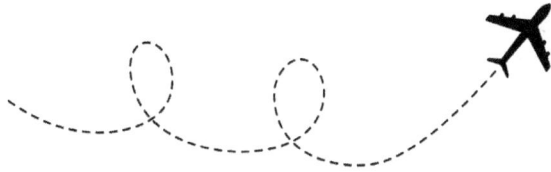

Whether it's diving into a fresh workout, picking up a new skill, or launching a side business, you might feel a burst of energy and enthusiasm as you take off and begin your journey. As you embark on your journey, think about how an airplane follows a flight path to reach its destination.

Think of a clear plan as your trusty roadmap—it helps you steer through challenges and stay on course to reach your goals. When you start with clear, well-defined goals, the journey instantly feels smoother. Break those big dreams into bite-sized steps, and before you know it, you'll be building momentum. Add a solid routine into the mix, and you've got the perfect recipe to keep moving forward with ease and confidence!

And as you face turbulence on your journey, remember to tap into your inner peace and focus, and stay open to the possibility of shifting your plan according to the circumstances. With a solid plan, regular steps, and support from your network, you can reach any goal you set for yourself.

Enjoy your journey—you've got this!

Boarding the Plane

Boarding the plane is when the journey truly begins—that moment when the doors close, and there's no turning back. You're committed to your destination, wherever it may lead. You've set your goal, prepared your "flight plan," and gathered all you need. Now, it's time to take off! Whether it's launching a business, switching careers, starting a new hobby, or moving to a new city, the key is to take that first step and trust in your plan.

So, here's the big question: Are you truly stepping onto the plane—embracing the journey? It's easy to watch from the airport lounge, pointing out what others could have done better, like a bystander critiquing a pilot's approach. But real success belongs to those who step onto the plane and face the ups and downs directly. The "frequent fliers" in life are the ones who dare to take risks, who don't always stick a smooth landing, and who may even hit turbulence now and then. But if you're staying in your comfort zone, you're missing out on the growth and discoveries that come with the journey.

You can't reach your destination if you don't board the plane. And let's be honest—if you're not encountering some turbulence or adjusting your course, are you truly challenging yourself? Playing it safe might feel comfortable, but it also keeps you grounded. So, buckle up, take off, and dare to explore new heights!

When I think of today's culture, especially my son's generation, there's a lot of encouragement just for "showing up." Don't get me wrong—it's great to arrive at the gate and see the plane outside of the window! But showing up is only one part of the picture. True achievement is the other half, and it's essential. Just like boarding a flight without ever taking off, participating without purpose can cause you to miss the opportunity for real growth and accomplishment. It's one thing to be at the gate, but it's another to push through, overcome, and actually reach your destination.

So, once you have your goals set, the key to being successful is focusing on the steps right in front of you. This is something the Navy SEALs teach, and long-distance runners know, too. I remember using this mindset when I was training for college soccer during pre-season. We had to run three miles in the summer heat, but instead of thinking about the entire distance, I'd focus on sprinting to the next tree, then jogging to the next, and so on. Breaking it down made the challenge feel manageable, allowing me to push myself further than I thought I could. The same principle applies when you're facing a goal or project that feels overwhelming—just focus on the next step, then the one after that.

When I'm engaged in a work project, or even the project of cleaning my home (which sometimes looks like a Tasmanian devil swept through it), I use this same principle, starting with one room and cleaning that, and then moving on to the next room. Not only does this give me momentum, but before I know it, I've completed the entire project.

I learned the importance of creating goals and taking action from my father. He grew up in a middle-class family, and when he was in high school, his father lost his job at a major department store. Suddenly, my dad found himself footing the bill for his college education. Fast forward 40 years, and my dad had transformed his entire financial situation. He amassed millions in investments, owned multiple properties, and we lived in an upper-class neighborhood just outside of Washington, DC. We attended some of the best private schools, all thanks to his relentless hard work and his partnership with my stepmother Ana, whom he married when I was 15.

My dad always told me, "You can do anything you put your mind to." For him, the planning was only the first thing. The most important part was getting into action. If I wanted some spending money, he'd challenge me: "You want candy money? Great! What are you going to do to earn it?" And let me tell you, I was out there on the corner of Woodstock Avenue and Covington Road, running my little lemonade stand with ice that melted faster than my profits. But those hot days sitting in the summer sun with my paper cups gave me the work ethic and resilience that has made me successful as an adult. I learned that opportunities don't just fall into your lap. If there's something you want, you need to act and make it happen—one cup of lemonade at a time!

ACTION PLAN EXERCISE
1. Take your list of milestones from the last chapter and reverse the order, with the final (latest) milestone at the top.
2. For each milestone, list the specific actions or tasks you need to complete to achieve this milestone.
3. For each task, estimate how long it will take.
4. Now, working backward from your milestone deadline, create sequential deadlines for each of the supporting actions. For example, complete one action before starting the next one.

High-Altitude Hack: You may want to give yourself extra "buffer" time in between milestones and/or actions so that if unexpected circumstances arise, you don't find yourself behind. On the other hand, don't overdo it; otherwise, you won't follow the plan. Try to find a balance to create a realistic plan that is attainable but also sustains your motivation to complete it.

SAMPLE ACTION PLAN
In this example, I will measure calendar days so that you're able to follow along. If this is a professional goal, you may want to count only workdays and skip weekends/holidays.
1. Launch the website by **November 5th**
   a. Announce the launch! *[1 hour]*
      i. **Deadline: November 5th**

    b. Conduct a final review of each page and test across devices *[2 days]*

      i. **Deadline: November 3rd** *(2 days before November 5th)*

2. Design and Upload a Portfolio Section by **November 2nd**

    a. Select the projects or examples you want to feature in your portfolio *[5 days]*

      i. **Deadline: October 28th** *(5 days before November 2nd)*

    b. Write brief descriptions for each portfolio item and gather images *[3 days]*

      i. **Deadline: October 25th** *(3 days before October 28th)*

    c. Upload/enter copy and content *[5 days]*

      i. Deadline: **October 20th** *(5 days before October 25th)*

3. Write Introductory Content for Main Pages by **October 19th**

    a. Draft engaging content for each main page *[10 days]*

      i. **Deadline: October 9th** *(10 days before October 19th)*

    b. Revise and edit the content *[4 days]*

      i. **Deadline: October 5th** *(4 days before October 9th)*

4. Create a Website Layout and Structure by **October 4th**

    a. Map out the main pages and sections of your website *[5 days]*

      i. **Deadline: September 30th** *(5 days before October 4th)*

    b. Choose a theme or template and customize it to fit your brand *[5 days]*

      i. **Deadline: September 25th** *(5 days before September 30th)*

5. Choose a Website Platform by **September 24th**

    a. Research and compare different website platforms based on your needs *[5 days]*

      i. **Deadline: September 19th** *(5 days before September 24th)*

    b. Test a few platforms by signing up for free trials or demos *[10 days]*

      i. **Deadline: September 9th** *(10 days before September 19th)*

By listing out each of the key actions and deadlines for each milestone, you'll be able to prepare and adjust your plan to complete your goal on time (or to adjust, when needed)!

Taking Flight

When you get your flight number, the plane already has a flight path mapped out—a route designed to get you to your destination while navigating weather patterns and wind currents for the smoothest journey. You're clear on what you want. You can see the big picture, like a movie of how your life will look. You've set your goals and broken them into clear objectives.

Now it's time for takeoff: it's an exciting, high-energy moment that requires focus and discipline to get off the ground and start your journey. Takeoff is just like starting something new—whether it's paying off debt, beginning a workout program, learning a skill, launching a side hustle, or rebuilding your life. It takes planning, commitment, and effort. But here's the good part: the momentum you create during takeoff will fuel your progress and keep you moving toward your goals.

So, how do you move forward and start taking steps toward those objectives? The answer is simple: identify the key actions that need to happen, assign resources and deadlines, and track your progress. And don't forget—you'll need to pivot and adjust your plan as life throws curveballs. You've learned many of these principles throughout this book, but now it's time to zoom in and break those goals into even smaller, more manageable steps.

One of my biggest lessons in overcoming obstacles and executing a solid plan came right after I graduated college. You know those college fairs? They're like a smorgasbord of opportunities! Well, Capital One showed up at St. Mary's College of Maryland with their shiny credit card booth, and let me tell you, I was sold. I thought, *Free money? Sign me up!* Little did I know that "free money" came with a delightful 29.99% interest rate. Yikes! Fast forward a bit, and I found myself drowning in $14,000 of debt on that one little card—without a single tangible thing to show for it. I wasn't exactly financing a car or a trip around the world. Nope, I was just living it up, buying drinks for everyone at the bar. Talk about reckless!

The situation escalated when my dad received a call from the bank about our joint checking account. Apparently, I had bounced a few checks. Now, my dad is not the kind of guy who takes bounced check fees lightly! Panic mode activated. He was worried about how my financial chaos might impact his credit. So, there I was, feeling utterly embarrassed and devastated. My dad stepped in with a stern but loving offer: He wouldn't pay off my debt outright, but he would help me learn how to manage it. And he doled out the "dad rules!"

First rule? Every Saturday at 9 a.m., I would come to his house for some financial advice and planning. Every Saturday, we'd sit down together, open the computer, and tackle that budget. Now, for a girl who cherished sleeping in until 11, this was a serious sacrifice! Every Saturday, we'd sit down together, open the computer, and tackle that budget. He laid down the game plan: Fill out a budget spreadsheet he would email me, and he'd give me a weekly allowance in cash. I thought, *What? Cash?* I had been living the high life with a credit card, spending freely. I received a total of $80 a week. Yes, $80! Can you believe it? Once my cash ran out, that was it. No more spending. This was going to be a real wake-up call!

And as we reviewed my expenses, it became clear that I had to move back in with him to save money —talk about a blow to my independence. I reluctantly agreed because I was desperate to get out of this mess. But here's the thing: Living at home made it possible for me to pay off that staggering $14,000, plus another $16,000 on a different card. As a recent college grad making about $40,000 a year, this was no small feat. But when you're not paying rent, and your stepmother is whipping up home-cooked meals, you realize there's a lot less to spend money on!

Using the snowball method, I tackled my debts one at a time. We started with the Capital One card and worked our way down. Each month, any extra cash I saved went straight toward the highest balance. Before I knew it, I was knocking those card balances out one by one.

My dad's approach was brilliant. He insisted we focus on that budget spreadsheet instead of my bank account balance. No distractions, just discipline and consistency. He taught me to concentrate on taking small steps that would "snowball" into results and create momentum to keep going! By the end of it, I had learned invaluable lessons about budgeting and using credit wisely—like using it for rewards or investments instead of splurging. But I had also learned an invaluable lesson about the power of momentum, as well as the power of community.

The following challenge is a great way to build momentum, taking small, daily steps toward your goal while celebrating every bit of progress.

THE SEVEN-DAY ACTION CHALLENGE
Step 1: Choose a Key Action
- Start by choosing one of the key actions that you added in the last chapter.

Step 2: Break It Down into Small Daily Actions
- Identify some small steps you can take each day to get closer to your goal. Make these tasks manageable enough to tackle in 15–30 minutes.
- For example, If your goal is to write a chapter, you could try "write 200 words," "make an outline," or "review what I wrote yesterday."

Step 3: Join the Seven-Day Challenge *(included as part of your exclusive bonus content, which you can access by scanning the QR code at the beginning and end of this book!)*
- Commit to doing one action each day for seven days. Grab a calendar or tracker to mark your days.

Flight Tip: Keep your actions the same every day, but keep them simple—this is all about consistency and having fun, not about being perfect!

Step 4: Treat Yourself with Daily Rewards

- Think of a little reward for yourself every day you complete your action. It could be something small like enjoying a coffee, taking a refreshing walk, or watching an episode of your favorite show.

> **Flight Tip:** Your reward doesn't need to be grand; it just needs to feel good to hit that daily goal!

Step 5: Reflect and Make Adjustments

- At the end of each day, take a moment to think about what went well, any bumps you hit along the way, and how you feel about your progress. If an action feels too hard, don't hesitate to break it down into even smaller steps.

> **Flight Tip:** Reflecting helps you see how far you've come and what really sparks your motivation!

Step 6: Review and Celebrate Your Progress

- Once you've completed the seven-day challenge, take a step back and admire what you've accomplished! Celebrate all the little wins, no matter how small they might seem.

Flight Tip: Let your success motivate you to keep moving forward—whether it's continuing your current actions or adding a bit more challenge!

Step 7: Repeat all steps of this challenge twice to create 21 days of momentum!

Remember to be patient with yourself. Small victories each day can lead to outstanding achievements over time. Studies have shown it takes 21 days to create a new habit and build momentum. The way to build lasting momentum is to take daily action and build upon it day after day. Enjoy the journey!

Climbing & Reaching Cruising Altitude

When a plane takes off, it works its way up into the sky, adjusting its speed and direction to find a clear path forward. This phase is all about making steady progress toward its destination.

In our own lives, reaching this "cruising altitude" symbolizes how we move forward after getting started. Now that we've begun our journey, it's important to keep pushing ahead and growing as we strive to achieve our goals. Finding that perfect balance in our efforts—where we feel confident and excel—can make all the difference.

My father always emphasized that simply showing up isn't enough; you need to fully commit to whatever you're doing. If you choose to take on a task, give it your best! This means putting in full effort, steering clear of quick fixes, and understanding that true success doesn't happen overnight.

That said, working hard without a clear purpose isn't the answer either. It's similar to baking a cake without icing—it may be a cake, but it lacks that extra joy. Success involves finding the right mix: you need to combine hard work with smart choices to make real progress. This is the stage where our dedication and careful planning come together. Our hard work starts to pay off, and we can move forward with steady progress toward our goals!

Think through your approach to your goal. Are you working smart *and* hard?

5-MINUTE REFLECTION:
INCREASING YOUR EFFICIENCY

Take a moment to reflect on your work.

1. Think about whether there are tasks you're doing that may not really be necessary.
   a. How can you simplify your work or delegate tasks that aren't making a significant difference?
2. Consider if there are ways to improve your skills or learn new things that could help you work more efficiently.

Tracking Your Progress

Just like pilots maintain communication with air traffic control while navigating, keeping a record of each milestone helps you stay aligned with your goals and ensures you don't veer off course. Each logged achievement serves as proof of your progress, reinforcing your commitment and providing valuable feedback that guides you on your journey, giving you a sense of accountability.

Moving toward your goal isn't just about reaching new heights; it's about constant forward movement, with each "crossed border" representing a specific goal you've achieved. Every milestone brings you closer to your ultimate dream, creating a path that keeps you inspired and motivated.

As you reach each milestone, take a moment to appreciate your accomplishments and reflect on the lessons you've learned. Each step contributes to your growth, making every milestone as meaningful as the final destination. The skills and resilience you gain along the way prepare you for future challenges and successes. With every "border" you cross, you're not just getting closer to your goal—you're becoming a more capable version of yourself, ready to achieve it.

Tracking your progress also helps you visualize how close you are to your goal. Each milestone reached serves as evidence of your advancement, and if your destination seems far away, looking back at what you've achieved can be incredibly motivating. Celebrating your past successes builds confidence and momentum for the exciting things ahead, even when challenges arise.

During long journeys, it's essential to remind yourself why you started. Each "country" traversed strengthens your commitment to your goals and helps you see the bigger picture. When times get tough, reflecting on all you've accomplished can provide the boost you need to keep going. Every milestone you achieve becomes a solid foundation, reinforcing your determination and resilience.

As you approach your destination, you'll feel a wonderful sense of satisfaction recognizing all that you've achieved. Just as entering a new country offers fresh perspectives, reaching each milestone allows you to appreciate how every step has contributed to your growth. This journey is about steady progress—not just giant leaps. When you finally reach your destination, you'll know that crossing each "country" and achieving every milestone was crucial to your success. This sense of fulfillment, knowing that every step was a thoughtful one, makes the journey just as rewarding as reaching the goal itself. Each milestone reminds you that success comes from consistent, deliberate effort, and that's truly worth celebrating!

Here are a few steps to help you track your progress:

1. **Take out the Schedule that you created in Part 2**
   a. Remember those milestones and deadlines that you entered into your calendar/schedule? Open that schedule now.

2. **Set a Regular Review Schedule**
   a. Plan a time to check your progress, ideally once a week or every two weeks. During this time, look at your goals and write down what you have done and any challenges you faced.

Flight Tip: During each check-in, ask yourself questions like, "What did I achieve this week?" or "What challenges did I face?" This helps you stay aware and make changes, if needed.

3. Reflect and Adjust Goals Your Goals, as Needed

    a. After your check-ins, consider whether your goals need to change.

        i. If you are ahead of your plan, you can set a new goal or adjust the timing.

        ii.If you are behind, you can revise your plan to catch up.

Flight Tip: Be flexible. Changing your goals does not signal failure; it is a way to stay realistic and keep moving forward.

Staying Calm During Turbulence

Turbulence during a flight can be a bit unsettling, even for those of us who travel often. It can catch us off guard and remind us that certain things are just beyond our control. But if you've flown enough, you know that turbulence usually doesn't last long. By staying calm and keeping our focus, we can handle those bumpy moments much better. This isn't just a handy tip for flying; it can also help us navigate the ups and downs in life by staying steady when things get a little rough.

Life throws its own kinds of turbulence at us, such as setbacks, disappointments, and unexpected twists. These challenges can make us feel shaken and a bit chaotic. In these moments, it's easy to panic or drift away from our goals. But if we take a deep breath and keep a clear head, we can think more clearly—just like trusting a skilled pilot to help us through a bumpy ride.

When turbulence hits, flight attendants and pilots remind us to buckle up, relax, and breathe. This advice works wonders for our personal lives, too. Taking a moment to ground ourselves, breathe deeply, and focus on the present can help us feel more in control. When we're calm, we can think through our options and make choices without being swept away by fear. Sure, life's challenges may feel overwhelming, but concentrating on small, manageable steps helps us keep moving forward.

Staying calm also teaches us to focus on what we can control. We can't change the weather during a flight, but we can certainly choose how we respond. Similarly, we may not control everything that happens to us in life, but we do have the power to decide how we react. This calmness is a valuable tool, enabling us to make choices that resonate with our values and long-term goals—even when we're uncomfortable in the moment.

BOX BREATHING EXERCISE

The Box Breathing Exercise, also known as "4x4 breathing," is a straightforward and effective way to help calm your mind and reduce stress. It's used by athletes, emergency responders, and military personnel to remain calm in tough situations. Oprah even uses this exercise when she's stressed!

1. **Get Comfortable:** Sit in a comfortable position with your back straight and your shoulders relaxed.
2. **Breathe In (Count to 4):** Gently breathe in through your nose for a slow count of 4. Fill your lungs completely.
3. **Hold Your Breath (Count to 4):** Keep the air in your lungs for another count of 4. Take this moment to feel calm.
4. **Breathe Out (Count to 4):** Slowly breathe out through your mouth for a count of 4, letting all the air out.
5. **Hold Again (Count to 4):** After you exhale, hold your breath for another count of 4 before you start again.

You can repeat this whole cycle four to six times or as needed. This exercise is perfect for grounding yourself before facing something stressful or when you want to stay calm and focused.

And just as turbulence eventually passes, life's difficulties often fade over time. By keeping our cool and staying focused, we become better at recognizing when things begin to improve and are ready to embrace the smoother times ahead. When we see our challenges as temporary hurdles in our journey, we remind ourselves that they're just part of life's ride. With a little patience and a steady focus on our goals, we can navigate even the trickiest situations and come out stronger on the other side.

No matter what comes our way—whether it's health issues, loss, or the everyday challenges we all face—we always have a choice in how we respond. We're not just passengers on this wild ride called life.

When I was eight months pregnant, I had just had a fantastic baby shower filled with laughter and joy. Then, out of the blue, my dad started feeling unwell. A bad headache and some balance issues led him to the doctor, and we received shocking news: He had stage four brain cancer. The prognosis was uncertain, with doctors giving him anywhere from three months to three years to live. What a whirlwind of emotions!

From that point on, we began discussing cancer survival rates. Some people might only live a few months, while many see around a year, and a small percentage might live three or four years. But my dad made a choice: He refused to let cancer define him. He faced treatment with incredible determination, trying everything from chemotherapy to acupuncture and natural remedies, all while working with a holistic doctor to make sure everything worked in tandem with his medical care.

Watching him and my stepmother Ana explore every possibility was truly inspiring. They went to counseling together and had some tough discussions about finances and planning for the future. Their bond was a beautiful display of emotional strength; they confronted difficult topics head-on. Dad was adamant about ensuring Ana was well taken care of, from their home to a new car, so she'd be okay after he was gone. I have so much admiration for caregivers like Ana, who show immense resilience in tough times. It's not easy to see a loved one decline, but they tackled everything together, trying to prepare for what lay ahead while still cherishing every moment.

And here's my take: If Dad had been dealing with a less aggressive form of cancer, I truly believe he could have beaten it. His positive outlook on life was remarkable, and he truly gave it his all. He taught me an important lesson, even at the end of his life, that it's not what happens in our lives but how we choose to respond to it that makes all the difference!

Mid-Flight Adjustments

To ensure they reach their destination safely, a pilot often needs to change their flight plan while in the air because of weather, other planes, or unexpected situations. This idea of making mid-flight adjustments is a fantastic way to think about setting and achieving goals in life. It really shows the importance of being flexible and adapting when challenges pop up.

Imagine you're starting at point A, which is where you begin, and you have your eyes set on point B as your goal. But as you work toward that goal, life might throw some curveballs your way that make it necessary to alter your approach. Sometimes, you might even need to rethink your goal altogether and come up with point C—an updated goal that feels more in line with what you truly want or need.

Just like a pilot who shifts their flight path to glide through turbulence, you have the power to adjust your strategy to keep moving toward your goals. This might mean changing your approach when a business plan isn't panning out or adjusting your timeline when life gets unexpected. It's about being resilient and adaptable. Remember, achieving meaningful goals isn't about perfection; it's about growing and evolving along the way. Whether you're picking up a new hobby, working on a project, or focusing on self-improvement, every step you take contributes to your journey toward success.

Life can definitely be unpredictable, and that's perfectly okay! Sometimes, despite your best efforts and careful planning, things just don't go as expected. It can feel like you're not making any progress, but trust me, it's completely normal to take a few steps back or sideways every now and then.

Think of your journey to success as a winding road filled with twists and turns. I learned this lesson in a big way while leading a team at Christian Dior. The corporate office brought me in to help guide a team of 100 people on a technology I thought I had all figured out. I had a detailed plan and was convinced that everything would go smoothly. Spoiler alert: It didn't!

My dad always told me to "prepare for the worst but hope for the best," so I had some strategies lined up. However, managing a huge international team proved to be quite a challenge. I quickly learned that I couldn't control everything and needed to embrace patience while honing my leadership skills. It was a valuable lesson in humility.

I remember chatting with Bruno, the Global Head of Sales, after about six months of this rollercoaster ride. I vented my frustrations, saying, "Bruno, this isn't working! The team isn't following my plan!" He smiled and replied, "Yvonne, you can't expect things to go in a straight line. You'll reach your goal, but it might mean going from Point A to Point C to reach Point B."

His words took me by surprise. I had been away from my son for two weeks each month for almost a year, thinking the team would meet my deadlines—but they weren't. Bruno gently reminded me, "You'll arrive, but it may take a little longer than you expected. In the meantime, enjoy the journey." That was a real wake-up call for me!

Up until that point, I thought success meant launching our project exactly on schedule. But Bruno showed me that success was more about teamwork and enjoying the process than just hitting every target.

All that to say, you might shine in one area of life, but that doesn't mean the same strategies will apply elsewhere. And something that worked previously might no longer work. Life's little surprises can lead you off course, and that's totally fine!

Here are some simple exercises to help you adjust your goals when you encounter challenges:

THE "FIVE WHYS" EXERCISE

1. When you run into a problem, try asking yourself, *Why?* five times.
2. For instance, if you're having a tough time with a specific part of your goal, start with, *Why am I struggling here?*
3. Once you have an answer, take that answer and ask, *Why?* again. Keep asking and answering *Why?* three more times.

This simple trick helps you dig down to the real issues behind your challenges and makes it easier to find solutions.

SWOT ANALYSIS EXERCISE

1. Grab a piece of paper and draw a big square, then divide it into four smaller squares.
2. Label them **Strengths, Weaknesses, Opportunities,** and **Threats.**

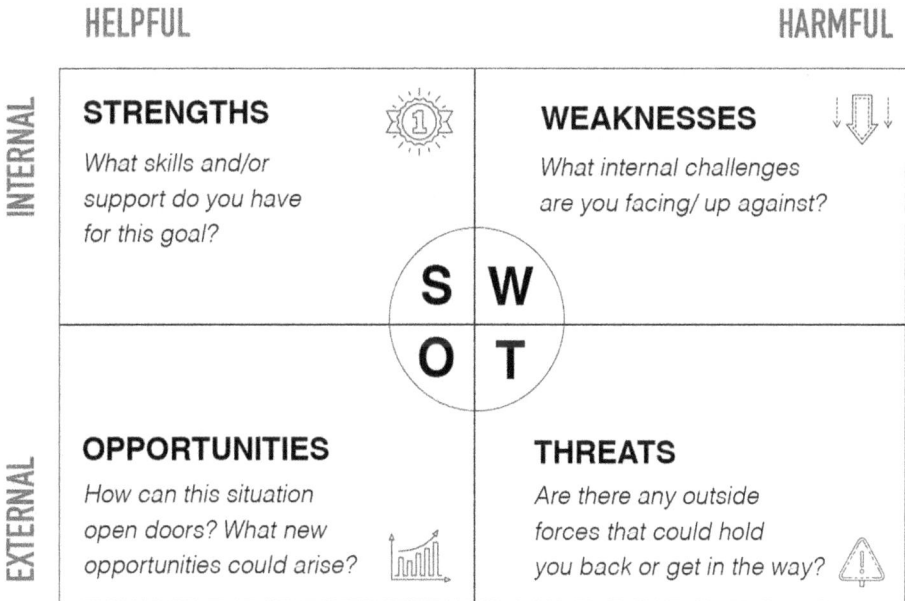

HELPFUL   HARMFUL

	STRENGTHS	WEAKNESSES
INTERNAL	What skills and/or support do you have for this goal?	What internal challenges are you facing/ up against?
	S | **W**	
	O | **T**	
EXTERNAL	OPPORTUNITIES How can this situation open doors? What new opportunities could arise?	THREATS Are there any outside forces that could hold you back or get in the way?

3. In each section, jot down three to five points.

    a.For example, in the Strengths box, write down skills or support you have; in the Weaknesses box, list the internal challenges you're up against.

    b.Think about new Opportunities that might spring from your current situation, and for Threats, note outside forces in your environment that may be holding you back or creating a toxic/unsupportive environment.

"WHAT IF" REFRAMING EXERCISE

1. Take a moment to write down the challenge you're facing, then come up with a bunch of "What if..." questions.

    a. For example, you could ask, "What if I focused on just one part of my goal for now?" or "What if I changed my timeline to make things easier?"

2. This approach sparks your creativity and opens your mind to new possibilities for tackling your problems.

With these simple exercises, you can uncover fresh insights and create a renewed action plan that helps you move forward with confidence!

Leveraging the Flight Crew

When pilots embark on a journey, they don't do it alone. There's an entire crew behind every flight, including co-pilots, flight attendants, and air traffic controllers. All of these crew members work together to make sure everything runs smoothly and safely. Just like them, we can also benefit from having our own "flight crew" when we're chasing big dreams. Mentors, coaches, friends, and accountability partners can play a huge role in turning our dreams into reality. With a support team by our side, we can tackle any challenge that comes our way, and this support team can change throughout the seasons of our lives.

Coaches and mentors are our air traffic controllers. They might not join us on our journey, but they have the big picture in mind. They can help us break our goals into bite-sized steps, keeping our "flight plan" organized and on point. Coaches are great at helping set clear targets and checking in so we stay focused and don't drift off course. They've been through similar situations and can share valuable insights. Regular check-ins with a mentor can help us avoid common pitfalls and keep us on track, providing practical tips that really help.

Our friends and family are a critical part of our support system, much like flight attendants who keep everything running smoothly. Their encouragement and joy lift us up during tough times, reminding us to stay strong as we navigate our journeys.

Accountability partners are like co-pilots sharing the controls with us! These partnerships involve mutual support through regular check-ins and motivating each other. They help us maintain our focus and work together toward our common goals.

Our broader network serves as an extended support team, providing advice, resources, and encouragement. Just like pilots communicate with ground control and other teams, reaching out to our network offers us fresh ideas and assistance. Every connection strengthens our journey and makes us more adaptable.

Having this support network creates an awesome feedback loop for reviewing our progress and making any necessary adjustments. Just as pilots constantly check their routes, regular meetings with mentors, coaches, and accountability partners help us see how we're doing and keep us on track.

Asking for help might feel a bit daunting, but it's really important for making progress. Challenges can seem overwhelming when we tackle them alone, but with a supportive team, we can face them with more confidence. Whether our goals are personal or professional, having trusted people around us makes tough times easier and inspires us to take bigger leaps.

Plus, a support network is fantastic for celebrating those little wins along the way. Just as the flight crew helps to serve us refreshments, our support system aids us in our progress, reminding us that our hard work is paying off and boosting our confidence.

While your journey is uniquely yours, the encouragement and insights from your support crew are invaluable. With mentors, friends, and accountability partners by your side, you have a solid team helping you conquer challenges and celebrate victories, bringing you closer to your dreams.

Building a reliable support network is essential for lasting success. Every step you take feels more rewarding with a trusted "flight crew" behind you, helping you stay focused and adaptable, even when the going gets tough. This team makes each milestone feel special and helps you keep your goals in sight, making the whole journey just as rewarding as reaching your destination.

Flight Tip: Don't forget to scan the QR code at the beginning or end of the book to unlock your exclusive access to **The Altitude Effect Tribe**, a community that will keep you inspired and accountable on your journey!

5-MINUTE REFLECTION: REVISITING YOUR SUPPORT SYSTEM

Review your "circle of support" and the people in your current network that you wrote down in Part 1 to support you in your vision.

- Are there any types of support that you are still missing to get to your destination?
- Are there people in your existing network that can provide that support?
- If not, how can you create that support for yourself? For example, do you need to join or create a new group of supporters, or strengthen any existing relationships?

Refreshments on the Flight: Celebrating Small Wins

On a long flight, there's something comforting and uplifting about the moment when refreshments are served. It provides a break, a chance to sip a drink or eat a snack, and to reflect on the journey so far. In the same way, recognizing and celebrating small achievements while working toward our goals can serve as those refreshing moments that keep us motivated. These little victories don't mean we've reached our destination yet, but they give us a taste of success, energizing us for what lies ahead.

Quick wins are like those refreshments. They bring us joy and encouragement during a long and sometimes tough journey. Acknowledging and celebrating these small successes can keep us engaged with our goals, rather than feeling overwhelmed or burned out. Each celebration allows us to look back at our accomplishments, reminding us that our hard work is paying off. Just as refreshments make a long flight more manageable, celebrating small victories helps us build momentum and maintain a positive attitude moving forward.

Taking time to celebrate doesn't mean we've lost focus on our main goal. Instead, it's a mindful way to acknowledge our progress, making the journey itself feel rewarding. Like a refreshing drink on a flight, these moments remind us of why we're on this path and what we've achieved. By regularly celebrating these wins, we create a sense of accomplishment that strengthens our commitment and helps us keep our energy up.

In the end, these quick wins and the celebrations that come with them are powerful motivators. They make us feel like we're moving forward, and each success—big or small—boosts our confidence. Just like refreshments lift our spirits during a flight, celebrating each step on our journey gives us renewed energy and allows us to face the next part of our journey with excitement and resilience. By taking the time to enjoy these moments, we focus not just on where we want to go but on the enriching experiences we gather along the way.

I remember the last thing Bruno ever told me: "Look at everything you've accomplished. Take time to celebrate your wins." That really stuck with me. I had been so focused on the things that didn't go as planned, that I forgot to celebrate all that I had achieved over the past eight months during that project. I had put processes in place, built a strong team, launched a pilot program, and played a major part in its international success. I realized that you don't have to wait until you've fully achieved your goal to celebrate. You can recognize and celebrate any "win" along the way. In fact, the more you celebrate the small wins, the more energy and motivation you create to help you through the tough times, especially at the start.

REWARDS EXERCISE

Use this simple exercise to celebrate your progress and make your journey more enjoyable. By combining daily rewards with rewards following each milestone, you give yourself something to look forward to.

1. Daily Rewards: Plan a small reward for each day that you complete an action towards your goal. This could be as simple as a coffee break, a short walk, or watching an episode of your favorite show.
2. Small Milestones: Treat yourself to something nice for each small milestone. For instance, reward yourself with your favorite activity or a special treat after a week of consistent effort.
3. Larger Milestones: For larger milestones, consider a bigger reward, like a massage or an item that's related to your goal.

By celebrating along the way, you can keep enjoying the journey while making meaningful progress!

Onboard Entertainment & Practicing Self-Care

When you're on a long flight, finding a good movie or show can be a wonderful way to relax and take your mind off the journey. In the same way, taking care of ourselves while pursuing our goals is super important! It allows us to pause, recharge, and truly enjoy the journey, making everything feel a bit easier and a lot more satisfying.

Self-care isn't just a one-time event; it's essential for staying strong and resilient. Think of it like picking a fun movie to watch—choosing self-care activities can bring us joy and relaxation. Simple things, like curling up with a book, meditating, getting some exercise, or even going for a stroll, can help us connect with ourselves, even while we're busy chasing our dreams. These little breaks aren't distractions; they're vital for keeping our minds sharp and reducing stress. They help us find balance so we can work hard without wearing ourselves out mentally.

When life gets tough—and let's be honest, it often does—making time for self-care becomes even more crucial. Just as you might watch a favorite movie or listen to your favorite song during a bumpy flight, we can turn to self-care when we face challenges and unexpected bumps on our path. Instead of pushing through, feeling frustrated or drained, taking a short break to recharge can help us regain our focus and tackle obstacles with renewed energy.

Taking care of yourself isn't a sign of weakness; it's actually a mark of strength and commitment. It's key to making consistent progress! Just like in-flight entertainment helps passengers enjoy a long journey, self-care activities help us avoid exhaustion and burnout. They remind us that the journey itself is important, not just reaching the destination. Self-care allows us to pause, breathe, and refocus so we can maintain our excitement and energy as we move toward our goals.

Self-care also helps us stay grounded in the present moment. Worrying too much about future goals can create anxiety and stress. In-flight entertainment allows passengers to relax instead of fretting about their arrival time. Similarly, self-care encourages us to savor the present, celebrate small victories, and appreciate every little step we take. This mindfulness makes the journey enjoyable instead of overwhelming.

You don't need to make self-care elaborate or time-consuming—it can be simple! Even small pleasures, like enjoying a tasty meal or a drink on a plane, can brighten our spirits. Self-care might be as easy as taking a quick 10-minute break, listening to some music, or chatting with a friend. While these acts of kindness toward ourselves may feel small, they add up and help us stay strong and focused. They remind us that while reaching our goals matters, taking care of ourselves is just as vital.

Incorporating self-care into our daily lives can keep us motivated! Just as a great playlist or a captivating book can make a long flight feel shorter, self-care can do the same for our journey. Knowing we have small, enjoyable activities lined up can lift our mood and help reduce stress. When we feel balanced and well-rested, we can think more clearly, boosting our creativity and problem-solving skills.

Lastly, self-care gives us the space to reflect on our progress without feeling stressed. Just like watching a movie during a flight helps you relax, taking time for yourself allows you to step back and see the bigger picture. These moments of reflection can help you recognize how far you've come, assess where you are, and make adjustments if needed. Self-care is an opportunity to look at your journey with excitement while maintaining a realistic perspective. It reminds us that the journey itself is all about growth, and every little step, challenge, and victory matters.

Flight Tip: As you continue on your path toward your goals, remember that self-care isn't a luxury—it's a necessity, just like enjoying a good movie on a long flight. These small, intentional breaks help us find balance and truly enjoy the experience instead of focusing solely on the destination. So go ahead—embrace self-care along the way!

WEEKLY SELF-CARE "DATE"

This exercise encourages relaxation and joy, giving you a creative outlet that can relax and refresh your mind.

1. Look at your calendar for the week ahead and find a one-hour slot where you can unwind without any interruptions.
2. Block that 1 hour in your calendar.
3. Use that hour to engage in a solo creative activity you enjoy, such as writing, drawing, playing music, or cooking your favorite meal.
a. Plan ahead and make sure you have everything you need (ingredients, supplies, environment).
4. The two most important parts of this exercise are that 1) you enjoy this by yourself, without kids, parents, partners, or friends, and 2) that you have fun.
5. Focus on truly enjoying the activity, rather than achieving a specific outcome.

Enjoying the View

You're on the airplane, flying high above the clouds. Sometimes, you may take a break from reading your book or watching a movie to look out the window. This simple act of looking outside helps you appreciate the world from a new vantage point. In the same way, when you work on your goals, taking a moment to feel thankful can help you see how far you've come and enjoy the journey itself.

Being grateful is like having a window seat on your journey to success. It allows you to appreciate the good times, find perspective during the difficult ones, and enjoy the little moments that make the experience enjoyable. With each glance out the window, you're reminded that reaching your goal is important, but so is enjoying every part of the journey. By embracing gratitude, you create a journey full of purpose and appreciation, making the end goal even sweeter.

When we set goals, we often focus intensely on reaching the destination quickly. While it's important to be dedicated, focusing too much on the finish line can make us miss the special moments along the way. Just like enjoying the view from the plane gives you a sense of wonder and calm, being grateful while you work on your goals helps you stay focused on the present, enjoy each step, and keep your motivation strong. Gratitude reminds you that success is not just about reaching the end but also about enjoying the whole journey.

Being thankful is a powerful way to stay balanced. Think of it as celebrating how far you've already traveled, instead of worrying about how far you still need to go. Every little success and lesson learned during your journey is important. Just as the scenery outside changes as the plane moves, your journey happens in stages. Taking time to notice how much you've accomplished helps you maintain a positive perspective, even when the end seems far away. Practicing gratitude can reduce anxiety and replace it with a feeling of achievement, reinforcing the value of your progress.

When working on a long-term goal, you might face challenges and obstacles. Sometimes, the outlook might seem unclear—moments of frustration or setbacks that make things harder. In these times, gratitude can help you stay steady. Taking a moment to appreciate even small things that are going well can help you get through tough times. Like finding a break in the clouds from your window, being grateful can shift your mindset so you focus on what's good rather than what's missing or going wrong.

Being thankful while working toward your goals doesn't mean ignoring problems or pretending everything is okay. It's about creating balance. In the same way that you notice both clear skies and clouds on a flight, gratitude helps you recognize your challenges while also valuing the positives. Acknowledging the people, resources, and opportunities that support you keeps you grounded and hopeful, helping you tackle obstacles with a clear mind and a strong heart. This balance between ambition and appreciation helps you avoid feeling burned out, letting you keep moving forward without feeling overwhelmed.

Gratitude also helps you stay present and prevents the "arrival fallacy"—the idea that you can only be happy when you reach your goal. The view from the airplane is beautiful even before you get to your destination, just as every part of your journey is worth enjoying. Practicing gratitude allows you to find joy in the process, making the journey just as fulfilling as the result. When you approach your goals with gratitude, you see that every moment and every small step is valuable.

Moreover, being grateful boosts your ability to recover from setbacks. When challenges come, it can be easy to feel down and out. But gratitude helps you refocus. By recognizing the support and strengths you have, you can face problems with more confidence and positivity. Just as a nice view can lift your spirits during a long flight, gratitude raises your mood and keeps you steady, helping you overcome challenges without losing sight of the bigger picture.

As you move forward with your goals, remember that looking out the window and practicing gratitude won't slow you down. Instead, it makes your journey richer, adding meaning to every step. Gratitude allows you to appreciate not just where you're heading but everything you experience along the way. By regularly pausing to enjoy the view, you're not only keeping track of progress but also celebrating it.

Gratitude is like a hidden superpower, and trust me, it's one you want in your toolkit! Not only does it boost our mood and emotional well-being, but it also helps us shift our focus from what we lack to all the amazing things we already have. Sure, goals are great for propelling us forward, but gratitude keeps us rooted in the present moment, making every step feel a bit sweeter.

And here's the fun twist: Gratitude can actually expand our success! It raises our vibrational frequency, attracting even more abundance and good vibes into our lives. Plus, it's something you can practice anytime, anywhere—whether you're thanking a team member, appreciating a loved one, or jotting down what you're thankful for.

I'm living proof of how powerful gratitude can be. My life could have taken a completely different turn, but I'm so grateful for my dad, who made tough choices that changed everything. His sacrifices shaped my journey, and I owe so much of my success to him.

Here are a few exercises that I perform on a regular basis to keep myself grounded in gratitude.

DAILY GRATITUDE EXERCISE

One way to incorporate gratitude is by taking daily "gratitude breaks." These breaks are your chance to metaphorically look out the window, take a breath, and appreciate what's going well.

• Each day, list three things you're grateful for that day—like a supportive friend, a productive workout, or a small accomplishment.

I do this exercise in the car each morning with my son, so you can get the entire family involved!

5-MINUTE REFLECTION: CELEBRATING HOW FAR YOU'VE COME

Another powerful gratitude practice is to reflect on past milestones and the progress you've made. Just like each mile on a flight represents how far you've flown, every milestone you've reached in your journey shows meaningful progress.

• Think back to a point when your goal seemed distant.

• Count all of the action items you've crossed off your list.

• Compare your current stats vs. when you started (weight, run time, budget, revenue).

Appreciating these milestones keeps you motivated, reinforcing the value of each step you've taken. It's easy to fixate on what's still ahead, but gratitude for past progress makes the journey more rewarding and the destination more achievable.

Summary

Congratulations—you've hit cruising altitude! In this chapter, you've learned how to maintain momentum and stay focused as you soar toward your goals. By setting milestones, celebrating quick wins, and staying adaptable, you've built the tools to navigate any turbulence with resilience and grace.

We explored the power of your "flight crew"—those key people who lift you up, keep you accountable, and help you refuel when energy runs low. You've also learned that progress isn't always a straight line, and that pivoting in the face of challenges doesn't mean failure—it means growth.

This stage of your journey has been all about building confidence, reinforcing your commitment, and ensuring that you stay aligned with your purpose. You're no longer just dreaming about your goals; you're actively making them a reality.

TRAVEL CHECKLIST

- ***Taking Flight & Creating Momentum:*** *Have you broken down your goal into small, manageable steps?*
- ***Climbing & Reaching Cruising Altitude:*** *Are you taking steady action and prioritizing your tasks?*
- *Staying Calm During Turbulence: How are you practicing patience and resilience when faced with challenges?*
- ***Mid-Flight Adjustments:*** *Are you open to making adjustments if faced with obstacles? How are you assessing and pivoting when needed?*
- ***Leveraging the Flight Crew:*** *Are you leveraging your support system? Where do you need more or different support to ensure success?*

- **Refreshments:** *What are you doing to celebrate your accomplishments, regardless of how small?*
- **Onboard Entertainment:** *What are you doing to practice self-care? Are you taking short breaks to recharge?*
- **Enjoying the View:** *What activities are you performing to stay centered and grounded? How are you incorporating gratitude into your daily life?*

As you prepare to move on to **Part 4**, it's time to zoom in on the final steps to bring your vision to life. The hardest work is behind you, and now it's about sticking the landing with intention and pride. Get ready—your destination is just ahead!

Part 4:
Arriving at Your Gate

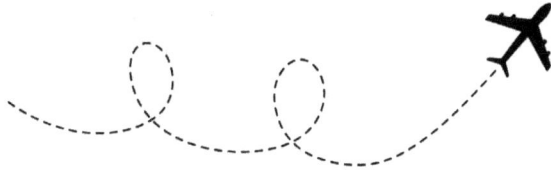

You've climbed, cruised, and weathered the turbulence—now it's time to focus on bringing your goal safely to the finish line. Every small action you take at this stage is crucial, and every detail matters. This is where focus and intention take center stage, ensuring that you finish not just strong, but with purpose. You've already done the hard work, so let's make sure this final stretch reflects the effort, resilience, and grit you've poured into your journey.

But let's not sugarcoat it—getting this close to the end can feel exhausting. You might be tempted to hit autopilot or throw in the towel, but this is your moment to dig deep. It's the perfect time to revisit your "why" and remind yourself of the purpose that started you on this path. Channel that determination, and use it as your fuel to carry you through the final steps.

In this chapter, you'll learn how to align everything for a smooth landing, fine-tune the details, and adapt to any last-minute surprises. It's not just about finishing the journey—it's about celebrating how far you've come and the incredible growth you've achieved along the way.

So buckle up, because this descent is all about focus, intention, and a triumphant touchdown. The runway is in sight, and it's time to land your goal with the same energy, precision, and confidence that got you here. Your destination is closer than ever—let's make it count!

Preparing for Your Descent

As the airplane gets closer to the ground, you start to zoom in on the details to prepare for landing. You can spot individual buildings, roads, and even people down below. When the plane is almost at the airport, it lines up with the runway to touch down. Every little action taken at this stage is crucial.

Descending is like reaching a personal goal—think of it as completing a project, hitting a health target, or achieving a career milestone. This phase is all about making sure everything is in place and that you are finishing what you started. You can't say a project is finished until it's fully done, or your goal is completely reached. You have to fine-tune the last details and ensure everything runs smoothly to safely land your goal.

It can be helpful to create a checklist to break down the remaining steps of your goal and help you stay focused on what's left to finish.

GOAL COMPLETION CHECKLIST EXERCISE

1. Jot down any tasks or actions that still need to be completed. Don't forget to include any last-minute tweaks or touches to really make everything shine.

2. To keep your goal on track and make sure nothing slips through the cracks, try setting deadlines for each of these final steps. You've got this!

Also, as you get closer to the end, it's natural to feel tired and want to throw in the towel. This is the moment to dig deep and remind yourself why you began this journey.

Reflecting on your purpose and your "Five Whys" can really help boost your motivation, especially when you're feeling a bit worn out.

REVISITING YOUR "FIVE WHYS" EXERCISE
- Take some time to think about your "Five Whys" for this goal.
- Come up with a short phrase or mantra that captures your "why."
- For example, "I am getting fit, so I have the energy to play basketball with my kids on weekends."

Keeping this motivation in mind can help reignite your determination when you need a little extra push!

Landing on the Runway

As you approach the final stages of your journey toward a goal, think of yourself as a pilot preparing for a crucial landing. These last few steps demand your complete focus and attention, just as a pilot meticulously touches a plane down safely. Achieving your goal means more than just arriving at the destination; it's about doing so with intention and recognizing the hard work you've completed along the way.

When pilots gear up for landing, they monitor critical aspects like speed and altitude, ensuring everything aligns perfectly. In the same way, completing your goal means paying attention to the tiny details that may have seemed trivial in the beginning. This involves reviewing your progress, double-checking your work, and making necessary adjustments to achieve your final outcome.

A smooth landing may also require the pilot to swiftly adapt to unexpected changes, whether it's shifts in wind or turbulence. As you near your goal, you might encounter last-minute challenges or minor setbacks. Embracing flexibility allows you to navigate these situations without compromising your momentum or work quality. Rather than viewing these changes as hurdles, consider them opportunities to learn and grow. Just as pilots trust their training to handle surprises, you can rely on the skills you've developed to deliver a strong finish.

As you finalize your goal, remember that how you finish truly matters. A well-executed completion brings a sense of pride and accomplishment, showcasing the effort you devoted to every stage and recognizing that you didn't just finish a task; you did so with purpose and care. Just as a smooth landing marks a pilot's skill, a strong finish reflects your commitment and hard work, setting the foundation for your next exciting adventure.

In those final moments of a flight, pilots do their best to descend gently, ensuring everyone onboard feels at ease. For you, this means wrapping up your project or goal in a way that leaves a positive impression on yourself and all those who will benefit from your efforts. Reflect on what "finishing strong" means to you—whether it's achieving a weight goal, publishing your book, or launching a website. Maintaining high standards up to the finish line demonstrates your dedication to both your work and the people who are supporting you.

Finally, when you've successfully landed, take a moment to celebrate! Yes, I admit, I'm one of those people who claps when the plane touches down! Celebrating isn't merely about marking the end of your project; it's about honoring all the effort and growth that brought you here. Pausing to appreciate your accomplishments boosts your confidence and reinforces your commitment to quality work. Whether you treat yourself, share your success with friends, or simply reflect on your journey, celebrating creates a memorable conclusion and clears the path for new challenges ahead!

Exiting the Plane & Clearing Customs

When you step off a plane after a long flight, it's a great time to think about your journey. You may feel a sense of accomplishment, reflecting on all you've experienced before you move on to new adventures. In the same way, when you reach a personal or professional goal, it's important to take a moment to reflect on that experience. Think about what went well and what you might do differently next time. This reflection helps you recognize your strengths, identify areas where you can grow, and discover unexpected lessons. By taking this time to think back, you can carry these insights with you, like essential items in your carry-on bag, ready for your next adventure.

Getting off the plane also represents moving from one experience to another. Each goal you achieve is part of a larger journey. The lessons you learn from one goal can become valuable tools for the next, boosting your confidence and expanding your skills. Embracing these insights strengthens you, making you more resilient and adaptable, so every journey prepares you for the next challenges and opportunities.

When you pass through customs, it's like getting ready for a new chapter in your life, whether that means starting a new job, aiming for another personal goal, or simply growing as a person. Just as customs checks what you bring into a new country, you should also consider what you're taking with you into your next journey. Customs officials check that everything is in order, which mirrors the importance of making sure you have the right skills and mindset to tackle new opportunities with confidence. This self-check is crucial. Before embracing new challenges, it's essential to ensure you're mentally, emotionally, and practically prepared for what's ahead.

When customs officers ask you questions, it can remind you to assess your own doubts and uncertainties. You need to be ready to answer these questions clearly, understanding your intentions as you move forward. Just like preparing for questions from customs, you should be ready to face any doubts or obstacles you encounter—this readiness is key to personal growth.

Sometimes, the beliefs or habits you've developed along the way might carry consequences, similar to having to pay a fee when bringing certain items into a country. It's important to take responsibility for your choices and learn from previous mistakes so you don't repeat them. Letting go of outdated ways of thinking is vital for your personal and career growth. Are your skills and habits supporting you, or do they need some adjustments? Reflecting on this helps you avoid repeating past mistakes.

Once you're able to let go of any beliefs or habits that are holding you back, you'll be "cleared" through customs! You've taken the time to reflect on your choices, let go of what no longer serves you, and are ready to embrace new opportunities ahead!

Here is an exercise that I've used in my personal and professional projects to create a sense of closure and allow me to apply those lessons to the future.

GOAL COMPLETION CHECKLIST EXERCISE
1. What Worked?

    a. Take a moment to celebrate the specific actions and/or strategies that contributed to your success. For example, "Breaking my job search into smaller weekly tasks really helped me to stay on track."

    b. Take a moment to acknowledge the progress you've made and rejoice in your achievements, regardless of their size.

2. What Didn't Work?

    a. Without criticizing or blaming yourself / others, write down the challenges you encountered along your journey and what did not go as expected.

        i. For example, "I underestimated the time required for certain activities."

3. What Did You Learn?

    a. For each success and challenge, document the important lessons you've gained.

        i. For example, "What did this experience teach me about achieving my goals? Are there any recurring themes or areas for growth?"

4. What Could You Do Differently Next Time?

    a. With your lessons in mind, outline three to five concrete, clear, and realistic actions or habits you want to adopt for your upcoming goals.

Summary

YOU DID IT! You created a goal, made a plan, and executed it! You drew upon your strength, resilience, patience, and fortitude. You may be tempted to rush off and quickly move to your next destination, but remember to take time to reflect on what you learned so that you can apply it to your next journey!

TRAVEL CHECKLIST

- ***Preparing for Your Descent:*** *Have you tracked and checked for the last-minute activities that need to happen to complete your goal? If exhaustion has set in, have you reconnected to your "Why" and ensured you have the motivation and stamina to complete your goal?*

- ***Landing on the Runway:*** *Have you made any necessary adjustments to achieve your final outcome despite what life has thrown at you? Have you taken a moment to CELEBRATE your achievement privately and publicly?*

- ***Exiting the Plane & Clearing Customs:*** *Have you taken time to reflect on what you learned and gained on this journey? Have you let go of any limiting beliefs or habits that are holding you back from moving forward with power and confidence?*

Okay, you may be wondering… that's all well and good, but what do I do if I face overwhelming obstacles? What if my plan crashes and burns? What if nothing goes according to plan?

Don't worry! Stick around for **Part 5.**

Part 5:
Overcoming Challenges

Let's face it: As we travel through life, there are many times when things don't go according to plan. Your flight is delayed, rerouted, or canceled altogether. Or worse—a plane crashes. These situations can be frustrating and, sometimes, downright terrifying. But just as these challenges are a possibility of any journey, setbacks and obstacles are often on the path to achieving your goals. These moments can feel daunting or overwhelming, but they also offer valuable opportunities to pause, regroup, and adapt.

Just as a savvy traveler learns to navigate these disruptions with flexibility and patience, embracing these unexpected changes in your journey toward your goals can create resilience, reveal new paths, and ultimately make the destination even more meaningful.

"Failing" to Achieve Your Goals

Not achieving a personal or professional goal can feel like a plane crashing just as it was soaring toward its destination, a jarring and sudden end to something that you invested so much hope and effort into. In the wake of this "crash," it's natural to feel disappointed, as though all the time, energy, and planning have been wasted.

When you fail, it can be confusing, and you might start to doubt yourself and your choices. But a setback doesn't mean you're not capable; it shows you areas that you need to focus on more. Just like pilots look back at data after a problem to see what went wrong, you can analyze your situation to see what didn't align with your plans. Taking a moment to reflect can give you important insights that help you recognize patterns or decisions that led to the result.

After a setback, pilots often make changes to improve safety, learning from their experiences to avoid making the same mistakes again. You can do the same by reviewing your unachieved goal and making adjustments. If you didn't reach your goal, it might mean that you missed something important—like not planning sufficiently, going too fast, or having unrealistic expectations. Maybe the goal was too big, you didn't have enough support, or perhaps you needed better ways to handle stress or manage your time. This reflection can transform a painful experience into a valuable lesson that prepares you for future efforts. Instead of seeing a setback as a complete failure, think of it as a necessary part of your journey. This helps you gather the knowledge and confidence to tackle your next goal.

Although setbacks can feel scary, they don't mean your journey is over. Failure, though difficult, can be an important avenue for growth and change. Just like a pilot who has gone through a crash learns to appreciate flying more, you can gain a better understanding of yourself and how you approach your goals. Bouncing back after a setback means making the necessary changes and moving forward with renewed strength. With the right mindset, you can turn a crash into a valuable lesson, using that experience to aim even higher in the future.

My dad always believed in learning from mistakes, and he encouraged us to embrace our failures from a young age. For example, when we were learning to ice skate, he would cheer us on and say, "Fall. Get it out of the way!" We thought he was a bit crazy, but he understood that falling—and failing—was a part of the journey. He didn't want us to be afraid of it but instead encouraged us to embrace the fear and tackle it head-on.

Even now, as I'm writing my book and feeling the pressure to be perfect, I often have to remind myself of my dad's wisdom. One of my favorite memories is from one of our beach vacations. I loved windsurfing, even though I spent most of my time in the water! Out of a 30-minute session, I'd be face-down in the waves for about 25 minutes. My dad would chuckle, his eyes twinkling with respect for my persistence. I never just gave up and said, "Forget it. Let's call it a day!" Nope! I kept at it, and that unspoken bond we had was built on mutual respect.

So, my dad taught me a crucial lesson: Learn how to fall, and when you do, don't just sit there feeling sorry for yourself. Get back up! Keep getting back up! Even if it's for 25 of the 30-minute windsurfing lessons you've paid for. Whether you achieve your goal or learn something valuable about yourself, at least you'll have that memory of giving it your all.

Life's all about those little bumps and bruises along the way—so embrace them! You never know what you'll learn or how you'll grow. And regardless of whether you achieved your goal or didn't, you'll always have lessons and learnings that you can take for the future. In fact, the lessons you learn from failing might stick with you even more than the lessons you learn from succeeding.

Sometimes you'll look back on the best times of your life and find that they are also the worst, and vice versa. Some of your greatest successes can also be your greatest lessons and "failures." All that you can do is learn from your actions and make a decision to move forward. Commit to learning from the experience and becoming a better person. Dig deep and reconnect to your purpose and your values, and remember that no one is perfect. We're all just doing the best we can. You will bounce back stronger than before, with new wisdom and strength for the next adventure. As for right now, be gentle with yourself as you mourn the loss of that dream.

Missing Your Flight

Missing a flight is a frustrating experience, often accompanied by a sense of regret and a flurry of "if only" thoughts: If only you'd left a little earlier, packed a bit faster, or planned for the unexpected. Whether it's an ambitious project that didn't quite come together, a deadline that slipped by, or a vision that fell short, it leaves you stranded with the lingering question of what went wrong. You're left replaying the missed steps, unexpected delays, and moments of hesitation that contributed to the outcome. The disappointment is real, and sometimes it feels like that goal is now just out of reach.

But just like you'd regroup and book the next available flight, missing a goal gives you a chance to recalibrate and learn. There's a space left by that missed milestone where you can pause and reflect on what kept you grounded and how you can navigate differently next time. Did you underestimate the time required? Overlook a key task? Fail to account for setbacks? By reflecting on these factors, you set yourself up to "catch the next flight"—a fresh chance to reach your destination with valuable insights and a new approach. Missing a flight isn't the end of your journey, and neither is missing a milestone. It's a chance to reset, refocus, and prepare to move forward with greater resilience.

My father was a master of giving grace—to himself and to everyone around him. He'd often say, "Failure isn't a bad word; it's just a stepping stone." Sometimes, you need to "fail" to shake yourself out of your comfort zone. After all, if everything goes exactly as planned, where's the growth? My dad, an entrepreneur who started multiple businesses, saw both success and setbacks. But he never let a failed attempt stop him from trying again.

One of the first lessons he taught me was to release rigid expectations about what success should look like. When we box our dreams into rigid ideas, we close off other possibilities. Sometimes, what looks like failure opens doors to something greater! Think about it: some of the world's best inventions, like penicillin, came from experiments that didn't go as expected. So instead of stressing over mistakes and missed milestones, focus on taking responsibility for your choices and learning from them.

As my dad would say, "If you're in a hole, stop digging!" Take responsibility, look in the mirror, and own your part in the process. Taking responsibility and handling setbacks with integrity defines who you are. These moments are golden opportunities to showcase your values, even when the going gets tough. Admitting a mistake and accepting responsibility shows your true strength and character. We all mess up, and sometimes those mistakes feel monumental. But true character shines through when we handle those moments with grace. So, the next time you "miss your flight," see it as an invitation to grow, learn from your choices, and embrace the journey with fresh perspective and determination!

Delays/Cancellations

So, here you are at the airport, bags packed, boarding pass in hand, and fully prepared to take off toward your destination. You've put in the time, the planning, and the energy, feeling ready to go. But just as you're about to board, you get the news: Your flight is delayed—or worse, canceled! It's a gut-punch moment, especially when you've already invested so much. You feel stranded, wondering how you're going to regroup and still reach your destination.

This situation mirrors the setbacks we face in our personal and professional lives. Despite all our efforts, things don't always go according to plan, and suddenly, we're forced to recalibrate. It's discouraging to be thrown off course, but it can also be an invitation to find a new way forward. When we face a setback like this, it's natural to feel like we're back at square one. But in reality, you're never truly starting over. Every step you've taken, every lesson learned, and every bit of effort you've put in has brought you valuable experience that you can carry forward. Just because your "flight" is delayed or canceled doesn't mean your journey is over. It simply means you might need to take a different route, one that offers fresh perspectives, builds resilience, and helps you approach your goal with new insights.

So, if you find yourself leaving a job, relationship, or any situation, remember: You're not starting from scratch. You're bringing along a wealth of lessons learned, skills acquired, and hard-won wisdom from the obstacles you've faced. Trust me, as someone who's hired and interviewed countless people, I know that hiring managers, recruiters, and clients are much more interested in how your skills can benefit them than in the details of your past. Recall Sarah, who we discussed earlier in Part 1. She's feeling stuck in a job that leaves her disempowered, but if she decides to switch companies or even fields, she's not leaving empty-handed. Those experiences have equipped her with the skills and insight to understand what truly matters to her in her career. Similarly, when it comes to finding a new partner, they're far more interested in how you've grown and what you've learned than in the specifics of your past. It's about what you bring to the table.

And if you're in a spot where you're feeling unsure about your skills or want to boost your marketability, you can change that, too! I remember feeling a bit uncertain even after a decade as a project manager, so I took six months to earn my Project Management Professional (PMP) certificate. It opened a world of new opportunities for me. Sometimes, just earning a certification or taking a class can give you the confidence and skills you need to take that next big step.

Dealing with setbacks requires patience, flexibility, and the resilience to keep moving forward. You're not losing the time and energy you've invested—you're adding to your toolkit for the journey ahead. Because even when the route changes, the journey continues. And through it all, you'll come out stronger, with a deeper understanding of what it means to persevere. So, when things go wrong, stay adaptable, keep your eyes open for alternative paths, and remember the progress you've made.

Layovers

Imagine you're mid-journey, and the pilot announces that due to low fuel or weather conditions, you need to land and are forced to have a layover. You're not at your final destination yet, and instead, you're waiting somewhere in between, perhaps with some frustration or impatience. In the same way, sometimes we have to pause a personal or professional goal—even if it wasn't part of the original plan. Life has a way of throwing us layovers, times when we need to hit pause on our progress, whether it's due to unexpected life events, new challenges, or simply the need for a break. While it might feel like your momentum has stalled, a layover can actually be a valuable time to recharge, reflect, and recalibrate.

A layover gives you a moment to consider your next steps, reassess your approach, or even discover new ideas you hadn't thought of at the beginning. Instead of feeling frustrated by the delay, you can use this time to gather new insights, sharpen your skills, or reconnect with the reasons you started the journey in the first place. Just as a layover can be an unexpected but refreshing pause before reaching your destination, delaying a goal doesn't mean abandoning it. Sometimes, a strategic pause can set you up for an even stronger takeoff when you're ready to move forward again. Embracing this layover mindset helps you make the most of every moment, so that when it's time to board again, you'll be even better prepared to reach your goal.

Everything happens for a reason—even if it doesn't always feel that way! In those moments when life throws curveballs, remember to look for the lessons and silver linings. They're there if you look hard enough. Take my experience with my father's cancer diagnosis, for example. At first, it felt like an unimaginable setback, but it became a blessing in disguise. Growing up, I sometimes felt resentful, thinking I was trapped by my dad's "rules." But his diagnosis gave us a precious gift: the chance to maximize the time we had left together and to truly deepen our relationship.

During those final days, our relationship blossomed. I even brought my collection of crystals from New York to his house during hospice—much to his amusement. There I was, trying to help him heal with quartz and amethyst while he chuckled at my "vibrational" remedies. That time allowed me to set aside my resentment and appreciate him for the sacrifices and lessons that shaped my success. To this day, my father's influence guides me, reminding me that while he may no longer be here in person, I'll always carry his wisdom and love with me. So embrace the journey, and remember: even "flight delays" and unexpected setbacks hold valuable lessons!

Summary

Whether you face a layover, delay, cancellation, or even a "crash" along your route toward your goals, there is always something that you can learn from it and take on your next journey. During those challenging moments, remember to leverage the mental and tactical tools that you've learned in this book. And most importantly, focus on your self-care and remember to give yourself grace. We're all doing the best we can with the knowledge and wisdom we have in this moment!

Conclusion

As we wrap up this journey through the metaphor of flights and goal-setting, I hope you've gained the tools to set bold goals, navigate obstacles, and savor every achievement along the way!

You now know how to turn setbacks into opportunities, celebrate small wins, and build resilience, setting you up for success in any journey you undertake. You've learned that taking off with a vision, crafting a solid plan, and navigating turbulence all contribute to the thrill of reaching your destination. Treat each step, each setback, and each success as an essential part of the journey, because every experience, whether you view it as a win or a lesson, moves you forward on your path in some way.

As I conclude this book, there's one last thing I want to leave you with: There's something even deeper to consider when defining success—achieving true **fulfillment**. Success isn't only about reaching a destination or ticking off goals; it's about living a life that reflects your values and purpose.

So, while the "A" in SMART Goals traditionally stands for "Achievable," why not take it a step further? Let your goals be not only achievable but also "Aligned" with your values. When your goals reflect what truly matters to you, they transform into more than just tasks—they become meaningful steps toward the life you want to live, a life filled with purpose and fulfillment!

Purpose and values are not static; they're dynamic, just like the journey. These elements will evolve as you do, and the journey itself will shift in meaning. With each goal, your understanding of what's important may change, revealing new layers within yourself. To live a truly fulfilling life, you need to be open to re-evaluating and realigning your purpose and values along the way.

So, as you reflect on the goals you set, remember that the ultimate destination is a life rich in love, connection, and purpose. Take time to cultivate these elements as you journey onward. Each goal you achieve is just one part of a larger, fulfilling life that values the people around you, the memories you create, and the love you share.

Connection, service, and love are central to a meaningful life. Without them, even the greatest accomplishments can feel hollow. Love isn't just about romantic or familial relationships; it's an energy that fuels us in everything we do. In my own life, I saw this with my father, whose sacrifices and acts of service taught me about a different kind of love. Today, as I juggle career and parenting, I'm learning how to balance the goals I chase with the love and attention my son needs. This balance teaches me that success in life isn't solely defined by external achievements—it's about nurturing relationships and living in alignment with my heart.

So, when you land at each milestone, celebrate not just what you've accomplished, but also the love and support that carried you there. Because in the end, true success is not just measured by reaching the finish line—it's found in the journey of a life well-lived, a life filled with love, purpose, and joy!

Acknowledgments

First and foremost, I have to thank God for my truly amazing life. Every day, I wake up even more grateful for the abundance of love, prosperity and joy that surrounds me.

To my family, especially Dad, Maureen, Ana, and Paul, thank you for the love, support and guidance that have made me into the person I am today. To Ty, thank you for being my inspiration to create miracles. To Cathy, Danilo, Pati, Erik, Rick and Emily, thank you for the extraordinary friendship and kindness that you showed Dad, especially in his final days. He was truly blessed to have friends like you.

Thank you to all my friends who have supported me along the way as I've picked up the pieces, who have cried with me, laughed with me, and toasted with me. To my 1311 crew, Cheryl, Dana, Dave, Donna, Dan and Jen, you helped me start my BK chapter. To my BK moms, Courtney, Melissa, Cami, Amy, Susie, Risa, Diane, Julie, Kelly, Janee, Makale, and Rose, you continue to inspire me with your positivity, vulnerability and courage.

To Brandon, Paul, Rose, and Ana-Paula, thank you for your willingness to read and endorse my book. I am so honored and grateful for your belief in me, and I appreciate it more than you know! To my Chief group, thank you for being my sounding board and supporting me on my journey to becoming an author. Kelly and Greg, thank you for being the first official members of my Altitude FX launch team. And finally, thank you to the Game Changer Publishing team, who have helped turn my dream of being an author into reality. I couldn't have done this without you!

THANK YOU FOR READING MY BOOK!

Unleash Your Potential with These Exclusive Bonus Gifts!

As my way of saying thank you for buying this book,
I've created a set of powerful resources to support you
as you pursue your boldest goals!

Scan the QR code below to access exclusive ready-to-use
worksheets/templates, inspiring video lessons, a guided 7-day challenge
to jumpstart your goals, AND private access
to a community built to help you win!

I appreciate your interest in my book and value your feedback as it helps me
improve future versions of this book. I would appreciate it if you could leave
your invaluable review on Amazon.com with your feedback.
Thank you!

www.ingramcontent.com/pod-product-compliance
Lightning Source LLC
Chambersburg PA
CBHW071444090426
42737CB00011B/1775